DILEMMAS
OF DEVELOPMENT
ASSISTANCE

DILEMMAS IN WORLD POLITICS

Series Editor

George A. Lopez, University of Notre Dame

Dilemmas in World Politics offers teachers and students of international relations a series of quality books on critical issues, trends, and regions in international politics. Each text examines a "real world" dilemma and is structured to cover the historical, theoretical, practical, and projected dimensions of its subject.

EDITORIAL BOARD

FORTHCOMING TITLES

Ted Robert Gurr and Barbara Harff
Ethnic Conflict in World Politics

□ □ □

Frederic S. Pearson
The Spread of Arms in the International System

□ □ □

Deborah J. Gerner
One Land, Two Peoples:
The Conflict over Palestine, second edition

□ □ □

Gareth Porter and Janet Welsh Brown
Global Environmental Politics, second edition

□ □ □

Bruce E. Moon
International Trade in the 1990s

□ □ □

Karen Mingst and Margaret P. Karns
The United Nations in the Post–Cold War Era

DILEMMAS
OF DEVELOPMENT
ASSISTANCE

■ ■ ■

The What, Why, and Who
of Foreign Aid

Sarah J. Tisch
WINROCK INTERNATIONAL

Michael B. Wallace
LOUIS BERGER INTERNATIONAL

Westview Press
BOULDER □ SAN FRANCISCO □ OXFORD

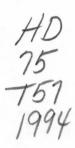

Dilemmas in World Politics Series

Copyright © 1994 by Westview Press, Inc.

Published in 1994 in the United States of America by Westview Press, Inc., 5500 Central Avenue, Boulder, Colorado 80301-2877, and in the United Kingdom by Westview Press, 36 Lonsdale Road, Summertown, Oxford OX2 7EW

Library of Congress Cataloging-in-Publication Data
Tisch, Sarah J.
Dilemmas of development assistance : the what, why and who of
  foreign aid / Sarah J. Tisch and Michael B. Wallace.
    p.   cm. — (Dilemmas in world politics)
  Includes bibliographical references and index.
  ISBN 0-8133-8408-7. — ISBN 0-8133-8409-5 (pbk.)
  1. Economic assistance.   I. Wallace, Michael B.   II. Title.
III. Series.
HD75.T57   1994
338.9'1—dc20
                                                                    93-27343
                                                                         CIP

Printed and bound in the United States of America

   The paper used in this publication meets the requirements
⊗ of the American National Standard for Permanence of Paper
   for Printed Library Materials Z39.48-1984.

10   9   8   7   6   5   4   3   2   1

To our parents,
Pirooz, and Tara

Contents

□ □ □

Tables and Illustrations

□ □ □

Acknowledgments

We are grateful to many people for helping us bring this book into existence. George Lopez and Jennifer Knerr convinced us to write the book. We appreciate their recognition that such a book was needed and that we might try writing it.

Winrock International Institute for Agricultural Development provided funding for some of the time needed for writing. This book was written before Sarah began her assignment as a visiting scientist at the International Rice Research Institute. We are grateful to former President Robert Havener for his support. Enrique Ospina and Henk Knipscheer have been stalwart supporters, and we thank them for their enthusiasm and encouragement. Melissa Beck Yazman selected the photographs from the Winrock archives and her own collection. William Bentley and Richard Harwood provided helpful comments, and Joan Newton and Bonnie Clarke gave us key logistical support.

John Cool, Patrick Morgan, Lois Schipper, and Mark Ufkes read our early drafts and helped us improve the book at key stages—we hope we have captured some of their concerns.

Rose Bautista patiently listened to our ideas. Gerry Rixhon helped find references and encouraged us to finish the project. Lev Gonick read early outlines, cheered us on, and provided much-appreciated long-distance support, comments, and references.

Our daughter, Tara, was incredibly patient and forgiving while we wrote the book and she missed many weekends of fun with her parents. We are indebted to her.

We thank Brenda Markovitz for compiling and summarizing the Recommended Resources section, which lists videos on socioeconomic development, and Libby Barstow and Cheryl Carnahan of Westview Press for their masterful editing of our manuscript.

Finally, we thank our friends in South and Southeast Asia with whom we have had the pleasure of working. They have taught us much about living in rapidly changing conditions and about the differences and similarities among people—poor and rich, urban and rural, educated and uneducated, Western and non-Western.

We appreciate the encouragement we have received in writing this book from Winrock International, the International Rice Research Institute, and Louis Berger International, Inc. This book does not represent the views of any of these institutions. We take full responsibility for any inaccuracies in the text and hope the book stimulates further discussion about socioeconomic development assistance.

Sarah J. Tisch
Michael B. Wallace

□ □ □

Acronyms

ADB	Asian Development Bank
AKRSP	Aga Khan Rural Support Program
ASEAN	Association of Southeast Asian Nations
CARE	Cooperative for American Relief Everywhere
CGIAR	Consultative Group on International Agricultural Research
CIA	Central Intelligence Agency
CIDA	Canadian International Development Agency
CIMMYT	Centro Internacional de Mejoramiento de Maiz y Trigo
DAC	Development Assistance Committee
DANIDA	Danish International Development Agency
DENR	Department of Environment and Natural Resources
ECLA	Economic Commission for Latin America
ECOSOC	Economic and Social Council
EEC	European Economic Community
ESF	economic support funds
FAO	Food and Agriculture Organization
FY	fiscal year
GATT	General Agreement on Tariffs and Trade
GDP	gross domestic product
GNP	gross national product
GTZ	Deutsche Gesellschaft für Technische Zusammenarbeit (German Agency for Technical Cooperation)
HDI	Human Development Index
HMG	His Majesty's Government
HYV	high-yielding variety
IBRD	International Bank for Reconstruction and Development
IDA	International Development Association
IDRC	International Development Research Centre
IMF	International Monetary Fund
IRDP	integrated rural development project
IRRI	International Rice Research Institute
JICA	Japan International Cooperation Agency
NAM	Nonaligned Movement

NATO   North Atlantic Treaty Organization
NGO   nongovernmental organization
NIC   newly industrializing country
NORAD   Norwegian Agency for International Development
OAS   Organization of American States
ODA   official development assistance
OECD   Organization for Economic Cooperation and Development
OEEC   Organization for European Economic Cooperation
OPEC   Organization of Petroleum Exporting Countries
PACT   Private Agencies Cooperating Together
PCV   Peace Corps volunteer
PPP   purchasing power parity
PVO   private voluntary organization
SAARC   South Asian Association for Regional Cooperation
SADCC   Southern African Development Coordination Conference
SELA   Sistema Economico Latinoamericana
UAE   United Arab Emirates
UN   United Nations
UNCED   United Nations Conference on the Environment and Development
UNDP   United Nations Development Programme
UNESCO   United Nations Educational, Scientific and Cultural Organization
UNICEF   United Nations International Children's Emergency Fund
USAID   United States Agency for International Development
USSR   Union of Soviet Socialist Republics
VDO   voluntary development organization
WHO   World Health Organization
WID   women in development

ONE

□ □ □

Development Assistance Dilemmas

As a college senior, my thoughts on postcollege life became concrete: I wanted to be away from school. I had heard of the Peace Corps and decided to apply. I knew nothing of Nepal, but it seemed far away and different from anything I had ever known. Eight months later I was an agricultural extension agent in a small village a few miles north of the Nepal-India border. This was far away, and it was certainly different from anything I had ever known.

In the hot season, the wind blows dust across the fields and through the village. The land is parched and dry. Nothing grows. It is a time for building houses and getting married.

In the rainy season, the dust turns to mud, and travel is impossible. The rain brings life to the fields and color to the land. It is a time for planting.

In the dry season, the crops ripen. It is a time for harvesting and celebration.

In all seasons, life is hard. Twice a day, the average meal—some unleavened bread or rice (for the rich) and a bit of lentils or vegetable—provides barely enough calories to maintain health and not enough for nursing mothers or sick children. Chronic malnutrition is common, as the typical villager's diet includes fewer than 2,000 calories each day.

The nearest doctor is two hours away by bullock cart over a bumpy dirt road. Babies and mothers routinely die during childbirth. One in five infants dies before its first birthday. Nearly half of all children die before they are old enough to begin school.

Although this is one of the richest villages in this relatively well-off section of Nepal, the average villager has only two sets of clothes—one for daily use and one for special occasions. One new set of clothes is purchased each year for the Desain festival at harvest time. The poorest go barefoot, the poor wear plastic sandals, and only the wealthy can afford shoes for special occasions.

The local agricultural extension agent—who, with a high school diploma, is one of the best educated young men in the village—receives a salary of about twelve dollars each month. This is more than most villagers earn and is more cash than many see at one time in a year. The poorest half of the households own less than one-tenth of a hectare of land each;

1

Nepal in its regional setting. The Peters Projection is used because it consistently achieves accuracy of area representation for all parts of the world.

they must live on what little food their land can produce, supplemented perhaps by in-kind earnings from labor at planting and harvest times.

Although universal primary education is a national goal, regular school attendance is a luxury for the rich, and even then for only a few lucky males. Books are too expensive for all but a few villagers. The local primary school is a concrete structure with four classrooms that serves many nearby villages.

There are three tractors in the village and perhaps ten bicycles. There is no electricity, no telephone, no running water. There are three open wells, two hand pumps, and a pond at the edge of the village. Most houses are made of mud, with thatched roofs. Some are made of sun-dried brick, with clay tile roofs. A few are made of cement.

Of the 400 villagers, five have been to Kathmandu, the country's capital, once in their lives. To most villagers, Kathmandu is Nepal, and they live in Pakari Gaun, their village near the Indian border. The village and surrounding area comprises their known world. Their friends and families live within walking, bullock cart, or bicycling distance.

What does development mean in this village? Villagers do not debate the fine points of development definitions or models. Theirs is a world of few options and little choice. They cannot affect long-term outcomes in their own lives. They do not ask "What is development?" or "Why should a country develop?" People want to grow more food and have more clothes. They want to fulfill their family and social obligations—by having at least one son ("an heir and a spare"), by providing dowry for their daughters and securing dowry for their sons, and by properly performing the religious ceremonies that define the daily dimensions of life and death.

Villagers rarely see themselves as agents of change in their own environment. Rigid social hierarchy, exploitation by local elites, low incomes that leave little or nothing for savings and investments, and lack of opportunity for exposure to anything except their own and nearby villages all combine to limit the horizons of most villagers. The world is the way it is, determined by unseen forces far beyond the village. Expectations are simple and low.

In the village, change is seasonal and cyclical, with well-established patterns repeating themselves as the wheel of life turns. Linear change and long-term progress toward desired goals are not part of the average villager's experience. The concept of induced change is hardly known and more rarely understood. Fatalism is the accepted and expected perspective.

Even asking "Why?" is rare. In response to a persistent series of "Why?" questions, I was told by the most well educated young man in the village, "There is no why."

Villagers may be uneducated, but they are not stupid. Over the centuries, they have developed patterns of behavior that ensure individual and village survival. From their perspective, they lead rational lives.

The people in this village are individually unique, but the village itself is not. Other villagers in Asia, Africa, and Latin America live in different physical circumstances and under different political systems, but the basic conditions of life in this village are found all over the world. For most of the world's population, Hobbes's definition is still true: Life is nasty, brutish, and short.

Villages are not static, even without foreign development assistance. They have their own rhythms; the social, political, and cultural forces that are changing villages go unnoticed by short-term visitors. These forces are the cumulative products of individual reactions to the everyday problems people face in the changing physical and social contexts of village life.

Are villagers happy? They smile, make jokes, and play games. They sing and dance. In their own terms, they may be happy or sad, just as richer people may be happy or sad. One test of their condition is reflected in international migration statistics: Hundreds of thousands of people migrate from developing to developed countries each year, whereas only hundreds move in the opposite direction—and many of these moves are temporary.

As I sat in the houses of poor villagers, I was often consoled by the thought that my sojourn in the village was temporary, a short visit to another world. I could always go home if things got too rough, and in any case I would go home after two years of volunteer service.

And then I realized: These people are home.

Unprecedented resources and technology with which to solve food, health, and education problems exist in our world, yet more than one billion people live below international poverty standards. Food supplies fluctuate widely in many countries, health care is unknown in many rural villages, and in many countries most women cannot read. The world's wealth is unevenly distributed among countries, among ethnic groups within countries, among urban and rural dwellers, and among men and women. These well-known inequalities provoke both private and public responses. Privately, poor people try to improve their quality of life, and philanthropic rich people try to help them achieve this. On a wider social scale, many governments now view the overall reduction of inequality (both within and across countries) as an important public responsibility. Foreign **development assistance**—resources provided by rich countries to help poor countries improve their living standards—is an important tool used to help address some of these inequities.

With the resources and technology that are available to improve the quality of life, it seems only fair to provide equitable access to these goods and services to all people; this is one of the fundamental assumptions of the foreign-funded development paradigm. However, this assumption is frequently challenged by people who oppose the sociocultural and political disruptions that accompany the rapid change that can be stimulated by foreign assistance.

In the twentieth century, cooperation among rich and poor countries on issues that transcend national borders has become a primary feature of international relations. Social scientists and government officials debate the causes of poverty among and within nations and states and search for solutions to alleviate poverty and stimulate economic growth. In this book we address the dilemmas that arise when people and governments try to improve the quality of life through economic development.[1]

Dilemmas arise when circumstances require that choices be made among undesirable or contradictory alternatives. Dilemmas are complex problems and do not have precise solutions; there are no "right" answers to the questions that summarize them. Foreign development assistance leads to dilemmas, because not everyone can have everything at once, and choices must be made. Who should benefit from development efforts, and where and when and how? Not everyone agrees on the meaning and pur-

More than one billion people, like these Kenyan village children, live below international poverty standards. (Photo by Jim Curley, courtesy of Winrock International)

pose of development and certainly not on the objectives of development aid.

For centuries, wealthier countries have helped poorer countries "develop" through various means, toward diverse ends, and with wide-ranging results. Development benefits rich countries as well as poor, creating foreign markets and a stable international system in which markets can flourish. Foreign development aid may be primarily altruistic or selfish in purpose: Realism indicates that governments provide aid only if specific selfish political objectives can be achieved, whereas idealism holds that aid can have an altruistic moral basis—governments and philanthropic organizations have long provided aid for humanitarian ends. More radical theories claim that development aid is an instrument of control, used to perpetuate unequal social and political relations among and within the states of the world capitalist economic system.

Nevertheless, most people want socioeconomic development; unfortunately, no one knows exactly how to achieve it. Development involves many factors—capital resources, administrative capacity, individual and societal attitudes, people's participation, and a bit of luck. Few would argue that to develop is wrong, but how to develop, who should pay for development, and who should implement development projects are open

questions. We address these issues in the context of international development assistance funded by rich countries as it has been attempted since
World War II.

THREE DEVELOPMENT
ASSISTANCE DILEMMAS

Three dilemmas arise in the provision of foreign development assistance. We examine each in detail, using agricultural and natural resource
examples as illustrations. These dilemmas can be summarized in three
questions:

□ What is development? (the economic dilemma)
□ Why do countries help each other develop? (the political dilemma)
□ Who should implement development? (the individual dilemma)

Addressing these questions may provide insights into the multiple dimensions of foreign aid. The purpose of this book is to help students of international relations and economics understand the process of development assistance. Socioeconomic development is a complex process, not a
zero-sum game between rich and poor people or rich and poor countries.
Although development can be described in universal terms, it is specific
to each country, to each country's history, and even to regions within each
country.

Rich and poor countries exist side by side. More people and countries
are poor than are rich. Poor people live in rich countries, and rich people
are found in poor countries. Why do rich countries bother to help poor
countries develop? There are many viable explanations, ranging from
pure humanitarian motives to dark Machiavellian scenarios.

Defining, designing, funding, and implementing development projects
creates dilemmas for states, organizations, and individuals. Although
much development is economic, these dilemmas are inherently ethical
and political. This book is designed to help readers understand three dilemmas that arise during the process of externally funded socioeconomic
change.

In this book we often use countries as the units of analysis. Although it
is individual lives that are changed by development, these changes often
result from decisions made by country planners and leaders. The main actors in development assistance are governments, as both donors and recipients of aid.

In this book we focus on the politics of foreign development aid—the
practical meeting ground of economic development theory and international relations theory. **Descriptive economic development theory** seeks

to explain the incongruity of plenty amid poverty in the world economy, and **normative theory** attempts to prescribe how countries can advance from being poor to being rich. **International relations theory** attempts to analyze power relations among state and nonstate actors in the international system.

Both economic and international relations perspectives provide important—but incomplete—analyses of the development process. We use contributions from each field to help readers understand foreign development assistance through the three dilemmas that characterize most socioeconomic development efforts.

There are many kinds of **foreign aid** (financial or in-kind assistance provided by one country to another); funds are given for military, agricultural, industrial, health, educational, and infrastructure improvements. We focus here on socioeconomic development assistance, and most examples relate to agriculture or natural resources. This focus reflects our experience, but the main points are also relevant to other sectors.

Our theme is that foreign development assistance is a complex economic and political process and is not the result of single-minded development donors, recipient governments, and implementing organizations acting in concert to achieve clearly defined and agreed-upon program and project goals. The difficulty in a country's or person's advancing from poor to rich involves more than merely the technical difficulty of solving economic problems in agriculture, education, health, and infrastructure; improved human skills in management and problem solving are needed, enabling policies must be in place, and difficult political and ethical choices must be made.[2]

The process of development—particularly the interactions between its economic and social dimensions and between physical and human factors—is still not understood despite decades of research and billions of dollars invested in development efforts. The designing and funding of foreign-assisted development policies, programs, and projects are complicated by strategic international economic and political considerations and by difficult decisions as to who can best implement these activities.

Gaining an understanding of the complex interplay of economics and international relations in the context of foreign development assistance is important for students of world politics and development, as well as for practitioners. Both groups need to consider which kinds of aid seem to work and why others do not. In designing development assistance activities, investments must be carefully considered, beneficiaries identified, and multiple political and economic objectives balanced. Donor countries must balance political survival instincts with altruistic inclinations; both donors and recipients need to select the most effective people to imple-

In designing development assistance activities for areas such as these slums in Bhaktapur, Nepal, investments must be carefully considered, beneficiaries identified, and multiple political and economic objectives balanced. (Photo by Melissa Yazman, courtesy of Winrock International)

ment development aid activities. We attempt to help readers understand the complex dilemmas embodied in these considerations.

THE ECONOMIC DILEMMA: WHAT IS DEVELOPMENT?

What is socioeconomic development? Are its many dimensions equally important? **Socioeconomic development** (a complex process of improving people's lives) involves technology to increase the production and improve the distribution of goods and services and improvements in human skills to manage a developed economy as well as the quality of the environment and nature of the political system. It involves income, health, education, environmental quality, the use of technology, the nature of the political system, and participation in the process of development itself. In short, it involves all facets of life and the activities of all people.

The way in which development is defined has a profound effect on foreign development assistance budgets and project design. Donors and policymakers often have different perspectives than project implementors, whose views in turn differ from those of the poor villagers who are the intended project beneficiaries. The responsibility for defining development can become the power to affect the process and outcome of development activities.

How should development indicators—especially health, education, and health variables—be measured? Is development a process that initially benefits only a few well-off people, who then share these benefits with more disadvantaged classes and ethnic groups?

The definition of development must answer these questions by specifying which dimensions to include, how to measure these dimensions, and how to consider the distribution of achievements along these dimensions. Defining development is thus a difficult conceptual and technical problem. It also has practical implications: It is used to identify goals and the means to achieve them, and implementation determines who benefits from development aid activities.

It is difficult to measure achievements along the dimensions of development, particularly when the distribution of these achievements is taken into account. To complicate matters further, achievements along these dimensions do not follow a fixed pattern, and comparisons across countries are difficult. Which is more important, higher incomes or better health? Improved air and water quality or better education? Protected natural resources or higher industrial employment? Along any dimension, is it better to raise the average achievement or to improve the level of the least advantaged people in the population?

These descriptive questions have prescriptive counterparts. Different definitions lead to different descriptive models of development and thus to different prescriptions of how to develop. The questions are many, and few answers apply uniformly to all countries.

Increasing agricultural productivity, expanding and increasing the efficiency of the industrial sector, and increasing the complexity and distribution of services are all important economic objectives. These goals can be achieved through technological change, by promoting **human resource development** (investment in people's skills and abilities) and strengthening institutions, or by improving macroeconomic and social policies. Once development objectives are determined, governments must decide how to achieve these objectives. Foreign development assistance is often used in sectors deemed critical to economic growth (agriculture, infrastructure, industry) or considered to offer the greatest human payoff (health care, education, clean water systems).

Budget and human resource constraints usually limit a country's ability to develop all sectors or use all approaches simultaneously, so choices must be made. Equity (distribution) considerations complicate these choices, which might otherwise be viewed as technical problems in economic efficiency. These political dimensions transform economic problems into socioeconomic dilemmas.

This, then, is the domestic economic dilemma of socioeconomic development—to choose the definition and the means to achieve development in the face of difficult tradeoffs among potential beneficiaries.

THE POLITICAL DILEMMA: WHY DO COUNTRIES HELP EACH OTHER DEVELOP?

Why do rich countries help poorer countries develop? Is it more important for a government to improve its own public schools, build a road for a poor, friendly country, or provide child health care in a poorer, but less friendly, country? How can donor countries resolve conflicting political and humanitarian goals in providing foreign assistance?

The world includes rich and poor people and rich and poor countries. Most people want to improve their own standard of living, and many people want to help the poor. Likewise, most governments want to improve the welfare of their own citizens, and many try to help other states as well. Unfortunately, personal and national budgets limit individuals' and states' abilities to achieve all of their objectives, and hard choices result.

Donor governments face difficult choices in allocating development aid resources when their objectives diverge from those of recipient governments. Recipient governments must sometimes decide between receiving assistance and maintaining control over development policies and programs.

To be effective, development aid must be targeted for long-term projects that require patience in funding and implementation, even though donor countries and organizations frequently alter their aid budgets as domestic and international political priorities change. Development assistance is a source of frequent conflict between long-term humanitarian goals and short-term political objectives.

Donor governments give development aid as an end in itself (immediate disaster relief, for example), to achieve long-term humanitarian goals, and to achieve political goals. These goals may conflict, and the conflicts are compounded by issues of state survival, security, and sovereignty. These political issues transform already difficult domestic state budget problems into international relations dilemmas.

This is the international political dilemma of socioeconomic development—to choose between domestic welfare and foreign aid and between humanitarian and political goals in allocating foreign aid.

THE INDIVIDUAL DILEMMA:
WHO SHOULD IMPLEMENT DEVELOPMENT?

Can **expatriates** (people who work in foreign countries) or **nationals** (the citizens of a country) better implement development activities? How should men and women define their roles to achieve development goals? How should practitioners choose between expatriate technical competence and local empowerment and between traditional male-female roles and variations that may be more effective?

Before development activities can be carried out, someone must decide who will implement the activities, and choices must usually be made between expatriate and national individuals. Assessing technical competence is often complicated by diverging donor and recipient views of development goals. Also, donors often wish to control development activities, even though recipients can implement these activities themselves.

Selecting expatriate and national men and women to implement development activities is more than a question of administrative efficiency—it involves control and ownership of the development process and its products. These complicating political factors transform administrative problems into practical implementation dilemmas.

This, then, is the individual implementation dilemma of socioeconomic development—to choose between expatriates and national individuals and between men and women in allocating control of donor-funded development.

THE BOOK'S APPROACH

Each chapter begins with a village example from our personal experience in Nepal that provides a concrete illustration of the main points of a development dilemma. These main points, highlighted by a variety of examples, are then elaborated to indicate both their conceptual bases and their practical implications.

In Chapter 2 we discuss the multifaceted dimensions of development. We focus on the dilemma facing anyone who examines the human tradeoffs implicit in choosing a definition of development, particularly the expatriate and national economic planners who must encourage development while promoting equity.

In Chapter 3 we go on to discuss why richer countries help poorer countries develop. Here we address the dilemma facing foreign-affairs political strategists and development professionals who must simultaneously pursue political and humanitarian goals.

In Chapter 4 we analyze the roles of expatriate and national individuals and the roles of men and women in implementing development activities. We examine the dilemma faced by development practitioners who must balance donor and recipient government desires while implementing projects and programs.

In Chapter 5 we discuss a range of current development issues. This discussion ties together the issues raised in the preceding chapters: definitions of, and prescriptions for, economic development; the politics of development aid; and the individual character of development implementation.

TWO

□ □ □

The Economic Dilemma:
What Is Development?

As a Peace Corps volunteer (PCV), my qualifications included a B.A. in philosophy, plenty of youthful energy, and little technical skill. My responsibility was to "spread the Green Revolution," and I was assigned to work with the local junior technical assistant (village-level agricultural extension agent) to encourage farmers to use improved seeds for planting wheat and rice, to use chemical fertilizer, and to improve cultivation through practices such as sowing seed in lines. The mechanism by which farmers obtained seed and fertilizer was a community loan from the local branch of the national Agricultural Development Bank, to be repaid the following year.

 I often discussed the merits of using high-yielding variety (HYV) seed and chemical fertilizer with local farmers. I explained the advantages of the HYV seeds by relating the guarantees from the District Agricultural Development Office: If farmers followed the technical advice, IR-20 rice (developed at the International Rice Research Institute in the Philippines) was guaranteed to out-produce all other varieties. I knew this was an empty guarantee, because farmers would not be able to follow the technical advice. That would require controlled irrigation—which was unavailable or required pumps—pesticides, and sprayers to apply the pesticides, none of which they had and none of which they could afford. In short, the technical advice that must be put into practice to achieve these high yields could not, in the current state of village agriculture, be implemented.

 Green Revolution technology was supposed to be scale-neutral—equally advantageous for all farm sizes. A farmer with little land who used a little seed, a little fertilizer, and a little water at the right time would increase production in the same proportion as a farmer who used more seed, more fertilizer, and more water to grow rice on a large tract of land. However, access to inputs was not scale-neutral. Irrigation systems were often controlled by the wealthy farmers; poor farmers (the tail enders in these systems) had to wait their turns, and the poorest farmers were beyond the reach of local gravity-fed irrigation systems. Wealthy farmers could afford pesticides and the equipment needed to apply them. Small farmers had to rely on cooperative credit to obtain inputs; large farmers could secure credit on their own.

13

The average yields of the new HYV seeds were higher than those of traditional varieties, but the variation in yields was also greater; they sometimes produced less than traditional varieties if fertilizer, water, and pesticide were not applied on time. Villagers close to the edge of survival could not afford the risk of low yields in the hope of obtaining these higher average yields because they had insufficient savings to allow one bad year and their base was too small to take a chance on average gains.

I planted demonstration plots of wheat and rice to show the effect of using the HYV seeds and chemical fertilizer, and I noticed that villagers paid much more attention to their neighbors' results than to mine, even though I put signs on all the plots describing the type of seed and amount of fertilizer used. My knowledge was regarded as being from a book and not applicable to village conditions.

I received a salary of $50 each month, and an additional $75 was deposited in my bank account in the United States, for a total of $125. My counterpart received $12 each month and covered an area twice that of mine. My time horizon was two years, the standard period for volunteers, and my long-term future depended little on my success or failure. My counterpart would probably spend his entire career in the Department of Agriculture, and his future could depend largely on evaluations by his bureaucratic supervisors, his family ties, and his political skills within the government bureaucracy.

Like my counterpart, I talked almost exclusively to male farmers, even though women make many important agricultural decisions. Social constraints inhibited communication between men and women who are not related by blood or marriage. One day I encountered two women in the fields and asked for the name of one woman's husband to determine if he had already been contacted about seed and fertilizer loans. Unfortunately, I had not yet learned that women are not supposed to speak their husbands' names, so this conversation was frustrating for both sides.

During my two years in the village, the number of farmers using improved seeds and fertilizers doubled or tripled, and crop production likewise increased—but was that part of a trend that would have happened anyway? In the middle of that period the monsoon rains failed, rice planting was delayed by more than a month, and the rice harvest dropped. As a result, farmers who took loans were unable to repay them before the following rice season, and their debt increased, causing hardship for their families. Those with large farms could afford to repay their debts and obtain credit, but small-scale farmers relying on the cooperative credit mechanism were in a tight spot. Before this problem was resolved, my assignment ended, and I returned to the United States.

Village development occurs along many dimensions. I attempted to introduce an improved technology to solve the problem of insufficient food production. In the course of living in the village for two years, I also provided an example of life from a different society, with different individual and social values; the villagers offered me even more dramatic examples. In both my work and my personal life, I directly challenged their fatalistic perception of, and perspective on, human existence.

Improved technologies and exposure to less fatalistic attitudes both affect village life. Both are important for development. Exposure to village attitudes is also important for *expatriates working in development; without knowledge of villagers' perspectives, expatriates are unlikely to find acceptable solutions to village problems.*

When I left the village, I illustrated a key difference between expatriates and local citizens: Expatriates can go home—and escape the problems of development. Local citizens are already home—and have no respite from the poverty and disease that afflict their families and friends. Expatriates have choices and can exercise options with regard to their futures. Villagers are unable to effect control over their lives. Expatriates simply never have the same stake in the success or failure of development activities as do local villagers, however committed and dedicated they may be.

Every PCV's experience is unique, but many lessons can be generalized. A technical solution is found for a pervasive problem; it works sometimes but has (and creates) its own problems. The technical solution is introduced with the help of expatriates, who have no long-term personal stake in the outcome of their activities and who receive much higher salaries than those of their host country counterparts. Expatriate advice is lightly regarded by villagers, who have much more experience with local conditions. Communication is complicated by cross-cultural misunderstanding. The expatriates go home, leaving some villagers better off and others with more problems than before. This experience of development assistance is typical of many activities based on the Western (and dominant) model of foreign-aided development.

I n this book we address the dilemmas associated with development assistance. Before development assistance can be discussed, an understanding of economic development is needed. In this chapter we discuss the definition of development and the models countries use to develop.

The economic dilemma of development is summarized in the questions, What is economic development? and How do countries develop? These questions, and their answers, have both descriptive and prescriptive variants. One answer may simply document how countries have developed in the past; another may attempt to define how countries should develop in the present or the future.[1]

THE DIMENSIONS OF DEVELOPMENT

More than 5 billion rich and poor people live in more than 160 rich and poor countries worldwide.[2] Rich and poor people are not evenly distributed among countries. Per capita income in Switzerland is nearly $30,000 per year, over 100 times that in the 24 poorest countries of Africa and Asia.[3] The wealth of the richest individual is measured in billions of dollars, whereas that of the poorest is near zero. The gaps between rich and poor are enormous, and these gaps are widening.

The distribution of population can be summarized in an imaginary world of 100 people. Of the 100, 22 live in China, 16 in India, 18 in the rest

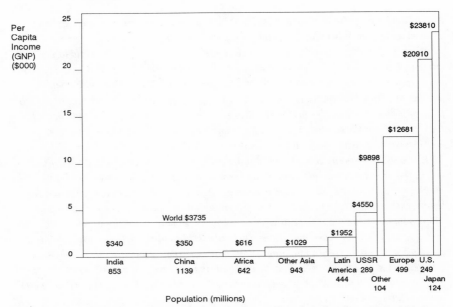

Per Capita Income (GNP) ($000)

Population (millions)

FIGURE 2.1   Population and per capita income. *Source:* Based on data from United Nations Development Programme (UNDP), *Human Development Report 1992* (New York: Oxford University Press, 1992), 98–100.

of Asia, 12 in Africa, 9 in Europe, 8 in Latin America, 6 in the former USSR, 5 in the United States, 2 in Japan, and 2 elsewhere (including Canada, the Middle East, Australia, New Zealand, and some Pacific Islands).[4] The world average annual per capita income is about $3,700; the range among these major countries and regions is from more than six times this amount (nearly $24,000) in Japan to less than one-tenth this amount ($340 and $350, respectively) in India and China (see Fig. 2.1). Most people in the world are poor.

Levels of health and education also vary widely among countries. **Life expectancy** (the average length of life) is over 78 years in Japan and over 75 years in 24 other countries, but it is under 50 years in 25 (4 Asian and 21 African) countries. **Adult literacy** (the ability to read and write) rates are 99 percent in 23 Western countries but are below 40 percent in 26 (mostly African) countries. Average **years of schooling** (the average duration of school attendance for people age 25 and above) ranges from over 12 years in the United States and Canada to less than one year in 21 poor countries.[5]

Equality is not dominant in today's world. Even the rate of population growth is unevenly distributed. As a whole, the world's population is growing at a rate of about 1.7 percent per year: The overall growth rate for the poorer **developing countries** (countries with low economic, health, and education levels) of Africa, Asia, and Latin America (the **Third World**) is 2.0 percent; whereas the richer **industrial countries** (countries with high economic, health, and education levels) have an average growth rate of 0.5 percent.[6] By the year 2000—less than a decade away—the world will have more than 6 billion people, nearly 5 billion of whom will live in developing countries. At current growth rates, the world's population will stabilize at 12 billion sometime near the year 2025, with 11 billion living in developing countries.[7]

What constitutes development in this world of economic disparity? Socioeconomic development involves improvements in food production, health services, education facilities, transportation and communication infrastructure, and markets for all of these goods and services. It often includes advances in industrial manufacturing capacity. Increasing food production requires seeds, fertilizers, water, cultivating and harvesting machines, and postharvest storage facilities; improving health services requires hospitals, diagnostic equipment, surgical tools, and medicines. Better education requires schools, books, laboratory equipment, and sports facilities. Improving transportation and communication infrastructure means building roads, railways, airports, and seaports and providing telephone lines and post offices. These physical achievements are necessary to improve human welfare and provide the foundations for modern economies.

Socioeconomic development also involves improved human skills to manage modern economies. Agronomists, nutritionists, marketing specialists, and social scientists are needed to improve food production; doctors, nurses, and medical scientists are required to improve preventive and curative health services; teachers are necessary to educate young people and adults; engineers and social scientists are needed to design and maintain transportation and communication networks; modern managers, salespeople, and accountants are necessary for efficient and competitive business; and policy analysts and administrators are required for public bureaucracies.

In addition, socioeconomic development involves opportunities. It includes the policy environment within which people and organizations conduct their professional and personal lives. These policies affect incentives related to both physical achievements and improvements in human skills.

Socioeconomic development consists of more than social and economic development; at its core is individual human transformation. For long-term social and economic change to occur, belief in the idea of individual and societal progress must replace the acceptance of fatalism.

There has been a tendency to focus on incomes in cross-country comparisons of development statistics. Income is easier to measure than are education, health, environmental quality, and political freedom. Implicit in this one-dimensional measurement is the assumption that achievements along other dimensions are correlated with income. As statistics on these other dimensions—particularly health and education—have improved, the weakness of this assumption has become apparent.

Socioeconomic development is not one-dimensional. It is not a single-faceted objective in which progress can be defined by one easily measured statistic, such as per capita income—which has long been popular as the yardstick of progress. Different kinds of development are important for different countries, which have different natural and human resource bases and different social and political structures. Irrigation is important in countries with little or seasonal rainfall; transportation infrastructure has different meanings for mountainous, flat, landlocked, and island topographical conditions; food production has different meanings in traditional Hindu (no beef) and Muslim (no pork) societies.

However, human beings do have similar needs and wants, so that the overall characteristics of development are generally recognized. These include high income levels, high literacy and numeracy rates, low infant mortality, long life expectancy, a clean environment, and political freedom.

Personal well-being is often defined in terms of income, education, health, and living environment. Likewise, the development of a society is often defined in terms of levels of income, agricultural production, educational attainment, health standards, and transportation and communication infrastructure; development goals are set accordingly. Measuring development is then an exercise in assessing a variety of achievements: per capita income levels and distribution; per capita food production; male and female literacy and years of schooling; male and female infant mortality and life expectancy; road, rail, and air networks; and telephone, radio, television, and newspaper communications.

This approach to defining socioeconomic development is fraught with difficulties. The quality of life is complex, and selecting a few (or even many) achievement levels as indicators of development can at best provide a limited view of individual or social well-being. Deciding what to include in development indicators is a difficult task. The World Bank and the United Nations Development Programme (UNDP) have worked for many years to develop reliable indicators of development. Per capita income, which in itself is difficult to measure in subsistence economies, is giving way to indices that explicitly include health, education, and other important dimensions. The World Bank *World Development Report* and the UNDP *Human Development Report* have dozens of tables and hundreds of indicators, many of which are further categorized. Are all of these indicators equally important? Even these long lists do not include environmental variables, such as air and water quality, or political variables, such as the existence of an elected government or the right of free speech.

Table 2.1 shows a few key variables for several categories of countries. One can see the wide variations among these countries and regions and the lack of clear correlation among the variables.

MEASUREMENT PROBLEMS

Even if there is consensus that the general definition of development should include income, education, and health, there are difficulties in measuring these indicators. Developing accurate—or even approximate—measurements of these quantities is not a simple task. How should in-kind compensation be valued in measuring income? Whose earnings are measured to determine family or household income—the husband's or the wife's? How should family labor be valued? In general, how should nontraded and public goods be valued? How should food consumption be measured—by caloric intake, including alcohol? Should protein and vitamins be included? Should literacy be defined as being able to write one's name or being able to read a newspaper? Should years of primary and secondary education be counted equally? Should school enrollment rates for males and females be reported separately? Is life expectancy a good measure of health, or should infant and child mortality and the incidence of disease be included?

In practice, income is usually calculated from **gross national product** (GNP) or **gross domestic product** (GDP). GNP is the total domestic and foreign output claimed by the residents of a country; it excludes intermediate goods (which are used up in the production of other goods). GDP is the total final output of goods and services produced by a country's economy, regardless of allocation between domestic and foreign claims. GNP is GDP plus incomes accruing to residents from foreign sources minus domestic incomes that accrue to persons abroad.[8] Expressing these magnitudes in terms of population averages gives per capita GNP and GDP. Unfortunately, using official exchange rates to convert national currency figures to U.S. dollars does not measure the domestic purchasing power of these currencies. The United Nations International Comparison Project has calculated **real GDP** using **purchasing power parities** (PPP) (an international measure of income that is based on its ability to purchase goods and services rather than on official exchange rates) instead of exchange rates. Real GDP—which measures domestic purchasing power—is internationally comparable.[9]

TABLE 2.1 Basic Indicators

Country Group	Area (million hectares)	Population (million) (1990)	Population Growth (%/year)	GNP Per Capita (1989$)	Life Expectancy (years)	Adult Literacy Rate (%)	Years of School (Age 25+)
China	933	1,139	1.3	350	70.1	73.3	4.8
India	297	853	2.0	340	59.1	48.2	2.4
Other Asia	1,124	943	2.1	1,029	61.2	66.8	3.9
Africa	2,865	642	3.0	616	53.7	53.2	1.8
Latin America	2,011	444	1.9	1,952	67.3	84.4	5.2
Europe	474	499	0.2	12,681	74.9	97.4	9.3
Former USSR	2,227	289	0.7	4,550	70.6	99.0	7.6
United States	917	249	0.7	20,910	75.9	99.0	12.3
Japan	38	124	0.4	23,810	78.6	99.0	10.7
Other[a]	2,049	104	2.2	9,898	69.7	79.1	7.4
World	12,935	5,286	1.7	3,735	65.5	72.2	5.0

[a]Includes Canada, the Middle East (Bahrain, Israel, Jordan, Kuwait, Lebanon, Oman, Qatar, Saudi Arabia, Syria, and the United Arab Emirates), Australia, New Zealand, Fiji, Samoa, the Solomon Islands, and Vanuatu.

Source: Based on data from UNDP, Human Development Report 1992 (New York: Oxford University Press, 1992), 98–100, 127–129, 170–173, 202–203.

Although GNP and PPP are highly correlated, the PPP measure of income indicates that disparities among countries are not so high as GNP statistics suggest. Per capita GNP ranges from only $80 in Mozambique to $29,880 in Switzerland; in 47 countries it is lower than $500, whereas in 10 countries it is higher than $20,000. However, per capita real GDP (PPP) ranges from $380 in Zaire to $23,798 in the United Arab Emirates (UAE); in only three countries (Ethiopia, Uganda, and Zaire) is it lower than $500, and in only two (the United States and the UAE) is it higher than $20,000.[10]

Health is typically summarized in terms of life expectancy, which captures a variety of factors related to disease and medical care. Education is often measured by adult literacy rates and average years of schooling.

However, development is more than the sum of income, health, education, and other components. Interaction among these parts can be as important as the parts themselves, and achievements in one area can affect the value of achievements in others. For example, increased literacy may simplify the dissemination of agricultural and health information and thereby hasten the achievement of increased food production and lower infant mortality. Sri Lanka illustrates the value of literacy in improving health; unfortunately, the civil war (politics) in that country has resulted in decreased food production.

People's local participation in achieving higher living standards is often critical to sustaining these achievements. Buying a fish with money received from selling petroleum is not the same as catching a fish at the local cooperatively managed fish farm. The fish farm is a sustainable effort using a renewable resource; petroleum is a nonrenewable resource.

Development is the process of a society moving from one form of social, political, and economic organization to another. In their critique of aid provided by the United States Agency for International Development (USAID), Lappe, Collins, and Kinley state: "Genuine development ... must involve change in the relationships among people, which in turn determine their access to productive resources. Development is not a technical but a social process, in which people join together to build economic and political institutions serving the interests of the majority."[11]

Development is also the process of individuals and institutions moving from one social, political, and economic perspective to another. These perspectives change from static to dynamic, from imposed to induced, from confining to empowering. Long-term development is self-sustaining by being self-capacitating for individuals, institutions, and society.

In practice, development may involve tradeoffs some people are unwilling to make. The pursuit of economic development often leads to changes in the social fabric, and countries may be unwilling to trade their cultural heritage for an improved economic standard of living. For example, women's traditional status in orthodox Muslim countries prevents them from participating in many public activities—often including education and health services and usually including professional income-producing activities.

Nevertheless, most countries have viewed economic development as a positive change and have made varying attempts (with varying success) to preserve their diverse social and cultural values as they pursue this change. Values and rituals often become confused when the social structure of a culture is confronted with rapid economic change. With the communications and information revolution of facsimile, television, videos, and cellular telephones, people continually receive information about other countries. In the face of this information onslaught, preserving cultural traditions (which is the source of many governments' strength) may be impossible. For example, Bhutan has enacted legislation that promotes traditional values, customs, and dress, but enforcement is difficult in the context of growing tourism and links with the rest of the world.

The quality of life can never be completely quantified. Even if individuals' everyday decisions implicitly assign values to many dimensions of life, people are often unwilling to make these tradeoffs explicit. Interpersonal utility comparisons are difficult, except concerning goods that are exchanged in formal markets; and many important dimensions of life, including environmental quality and political freedom, are not reflected in such markets. The definition of socioeconomic development has continually evolved, and the nature of the static and dynamic (both causal and coincidental) relationships among its various aspects (physical infrastructure, human resource development, and the policy environment) may never be entirely clear.

CROSS-COUNTRY COMPARISONS

Deciding how to measure development is even more difficult in making cross-country comparisons. Definitions of important concepts (such as literacy and what constitutes a household) vary from country to country, data collection and reporting methods and skills differ, and government recordkeeping is not uniform. Standardization of data across countries—a necessary basis for comparisons—is extremely difficult, especially when countries have different cultural values; for example, literacy is hard to measure in countries with strong oral and weak written educational traditions.

Many attempts have been made to construct indices of development to measure this process and to facilitate cross-country comparisons. Perhaps the most systematic of these is the **Human Development Index** (HDI), de-

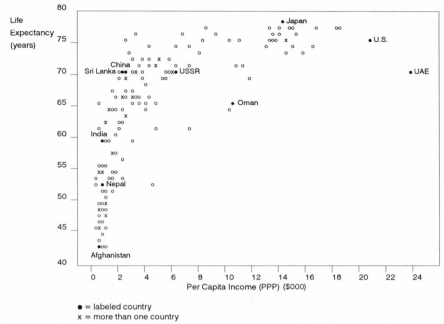

FIGURE 2.2 Income and life expectancy. *Source:* Based on data from United Nations Development Programme (UNDP), *Human Development Report 1992* (New York: Oxford University Press, 1992), 127–129.

vised by the United Nations Development Programme. Developers of all indices have faced the same questions: What indicators should be included? How should these indicators be measured? How much weight should be given to each indicator? The HDI is a composite index that includes income (purchasing power parity), health (life expectancy), and education (literacy and years of schooling); it is calculated by specifying minimum and desirable values for each indicator, indexing these endpoints, and averaging the three scales.[12] This is a considerable improvement over per capita income alone, the previous standard measure of development progress.

Although the components of the HDI—income, health, and education—are somewhat correlated, relations among them are not uniquely defined: Achievements along these dimensions do not necessarily move together. Figures 2.2, 2.3, and 2.4 show the two-way relationships between pairs of the three variables—income (purchasing power parity [PPP]), health (life expectancy), and education (literacy). The relationships between income and these health and education variables are obviously not

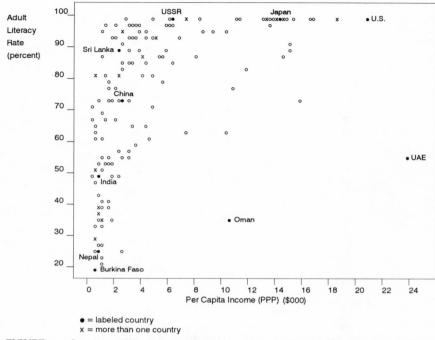

FIGURE 2.3   Income and literacy. *Source:* Based on data from United Nations Development Programme (UNDP), *Human Development Report 1992* (New York: Oxford University Press, 1992), 127–129.

linear (Figs. 2.2 and 2.3). Low income seems compatible with a wide range of life expectancies and literacy rates, whereas countries with high incomes usually have long life expectancies and high literacy. There are outliers in both directions: Some countries in the Middle East (such as the UAE and Oman) have high incomes and low literacy, and a few countries (such as Sri Lanka) have low incomes, high life expectancies, and high literacy. The situation in the Middle East may be explained by the relatively recent wealth of these countries—it takes longer to change education levels than it does to increase income.

Sri Lanka's per capita GNP is only $430 (real GDP is $2,253), but life expectancy is 71 years and literacy is 88 percent. Although the United Arab Emirates' per capita GNP is $18,430 (real GDP is $23,798) and life expectancy is 71 years, literacy is only 55 percent; Oman's literacy is also much lower than that of other countries with similar incomes.[13] The source and use of national income make a difference: Sri Lanka invested its meager income in social services and now enjoys high health and education stan-

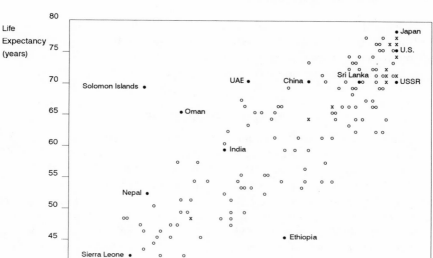

FIGURE 2.4   Literacy and life expectancy. *Source:* Based on data from United Nations Development Programme (UNDP), *Human Development Report 1992* (New York: Oxford University Press, 1992), 127–129.

dards; much of the income in the UAE and Oman comes from depleting nonrenewable petroleum resources rather than from utilizing complex human skills. Several Caribbean countries (Cuba, Dominica, and Jamaica) also have high life expectancies and literacy rates in combination with low incomes.

The relationship between literacy and life expectancy is more linear (see Fig. 2.4), with considerable variation around the average values. Even here there are outliers: Life expectancy in the Solomon Islands is almost 70 years, although the literacy rate is only 24 percent; life expectancy in Ethiopia is less than 46 years, but the literacy rate is 66 percent.[14]

The HDI does not capture all aspects of individual and social welfare. China and India have nearly identical per capita incomes ($350 and $340, respectively), but after these are adjusted for purchasing power parity (per capita real GDPs are $2,656 and $910) and health and education factors are considered, China's HDI (.612) is considerably higher than India's (.297).[15] Further, the HDI does not measure political freedom: India is the world's most populous democracy; China is the world's most populous authoritarian regime.

Measuring development plays an important role in evaluating the distributional effects of development activities. Distributional considerations affect donor decisions about providing aid and also affect both donor and recipient assessments of the effectiveness of development assistance.

DISTRIBUTIONAL ISSUES

Equity (distribution) considerations complicate development and development assistance; these might otherwise be viewed as technical problems in economic efficiency. The distribution of development assistance and its benefits result from conscious political choices for change or from decisions to preserve the status quo. The gains from development are never evenly distributed among the population—rich and poor, men and women, rural villagers and urban dwellers, ethnic groups, and young and old do not benefit equally. Rich people are usually in better positions than are poor people to benefit from the economic consequences of changes; concentrated urban dwellers wield more political power than scattered rural villagers; and organized voters benefit more than children do. Dominant religious and ethnic groups are also disproportionately advantaged.

This uneven distribution is sometimes the result of conscious political decisions: Funds for agricultural development may be allocated to a particular region as a reward or enticement for political support, past or anticipated. Sometimes uneven distribution is the unintended consequence of the technology of development: The improved seeds and chemical fertilizer of the **Green Revolution** (the modern technology for producing rice, maize, and wheat by using HYV seeds, fertilizer, and good water management developed at international research centers) were supposed to be scale-neutral and to increase food production for farmers with both large and small landholdings; however, access to the credit needed to obtain the seeds and fertilizers, and access to the irrigation facilities needed to provide water, were skewed toward the rich farmers, who benefited disproportionately as a result.[16] Sharecroppers often saw their options reduced as landowners increased their determination not to permit tenants to share in the rights of the land they cultivated.[17]

Deciding who should benefit from development assistance is difficult. Humanitarian-oriented donors focus on the disadvantaged, whereas politically motivated donors may wish to benefit other groups. Recipient governments usually seek to preserve the status quo and enhance their own power. From an ethical perspective, development should benefit two groups: the poorest people and those who are willing to work to uplift themselves. These two groups may not be identical. Unfortunately, the poorest people often have no time to do anything except provide for their

Sometimes uneven distribution is the unintended consequence of
the technology of development; here, women plant seeds in
Senegal. (Photo by Tom Osborne, courtesy of Winrock International)

own survival, and they often live in ecologically marginal places that are
extremely difficult to develop.

Not everyone is equally positioned to benefit from investments in economic development. For governments and donors looking for immedi-
ately measurable impacts, temptation often exists to extend development
benefits to those who are already relatively well-off in the belief that entrepreneurs will use their increased wealth to create opportunities, employment, goods, and services and that these benefits will trickle down to their
less fortunate neighbors. Unfortunately, this **trickle-down** process is often
slow and depends on social and political factors. In the meantime, the
gaps between rich and poor can widen considerably.[18]

These added ethical dimensions—deciding and designing who should or will benefit from foreign assistance in the face of competing political objectives—transform technical development problems into socioeconomic dilemmas.

Measuring Equity

If improvements in income, health, and education are important measures of development, the distribution of these achievements is also important for understanding the impact of foreign aid. If average per capita incomes are equal, is a country with both rich and poor people more or less developed than a country that has only middle-class citizens? Should gains by both poor and rich people be counted equally? Because much development assistance is focused on the distribution of economic and other achievements among disadvantaged groups, the share of the poorest 20 or 40 percent of a country's population is often used as a measure of distribution.

Among developing countries, the share of national income received by the poorest 40 percent of households varies from 8 percent in Brazil to more than 20 percent in Indonesia, Morocco, India, and Bangladesh; for industrialized countries, the range is from 16 percent in the United States, Australia, and New Zealand to more than 21 percent in Japan, Sweden, and Belgium and more than 24 percent in Poland and Hungary. The ratio of the income shares of the highest 20 percent and the lowest 20 percent of those within a country varies from 26 in Brazil to less than 5 in Indonesia, Morocco, and Bangladesh; for industrialized countries, the range is much narrower—from more than 8 in Switzerland, the United States, Australia, and New Zealand to less than 5 in Japan, Sweden, Belgium, Poland, and Hungary.[19] These figures illustrate the diversity in income ranges within rich and poor countries.

Gender Equity

One of the most important distributional aspects of socioeconomic development is the differential impact of foreign aid on men and women. This disparity has attracted the attention of donors, who question why the benefits of development are unequally distributed. Control of income, access to education, status of nutrition and health, and participation in politics can vary dramatically with gender. Income distribution within countries varies between men and women: If men are poor, women are poorer. Poverty is usually measured by income, and income is generated by employment. Even in developed countries, women's GDP is often less than half that of men's. For 33 countries with information on relative wage ratios and labor force participation, female incomes as a percentage of male

Female literacy and schooling levels are low both absolutely and relative to male levels; note all-male classroom in Nepal. (Photo by Richard Hawkins, courtesy of Winrock International)

incomes range from 26 percent (Costa Rica) to 82 percent (Sweden); this ratio is 49 percent in the United States and 34 percent in Japan.[20]

Literacy rates and years of schooling further illustrate gender disparities. Female literacy and schooling levels are low both absolutely and relative to male levels:

- □ In all developing countries except one (Venezuela), male literacy rates are higher than female rates.
- □ In more than 20 countries, male literacy is more than twice the level of female literacy.
- □ In more than 20 countries, the female literacy rate is below 25 percent.
- □ In only 8 (mostly Latin American) countries are years of schooling for females higher than for males.
- □ In more than 50 countries, males attend school more than twice as long as females.
- □ In 35 (mostly African) countries, the average duration of schooling for females is less than one year.[21]

TABLE 2.2 Gender Gaps in Literacy and Schooling

Country	Adult Literacy Rate (%)			Years of Schooling (Age 25+)		
	Total 1990	Male 1990	Female 1990	Total 1990	Male 1990	Female 1990
India	48	62	34	2.4	3.5	1.2
China	73	84	62	4.8	6.0	3.6
Developing countries	64	74	54	3.7	4.6	2.7

Source: Based on data from UNDP, *Human Development Report 1992* (New York: Oxford University Press, 1992), 136–137.

Table 2.2 shows literacy rates and years of schooling for China and India; these levels are typical of many developing countries.

Protection of the social status quo is also an important factor in allocation of and access to development resources. Differences between men and women in access to these benefits are culturally defined and enforced. Gender issues can transcend both race and ethnicity. The allocation of labor, sources of income, financial responsibility, and access to and control of resources are gender related. In most countries, men usually receive more benefits from formal development assistance activities than do women. Sometimes this uneven distribution is intentional, the result of cultural norms that prescribe gender-related roles for men and women. It is sometimes an unintended consequence of the nature of the technology involved. Recommendations to plant rice in rows will increase labor for the people who transplant the rice (usually women); donor-funded overseas graduate scholarships will benefit those who have already finished undergraduate degrees and have learned English (mostly men).

Socioeconomic development affects men and women differently. Even though advances in food production and natural resource management often cannot be made without the participation of rural women, the development trickles down to women through patriarchal social structures at the village and national levels. Women are key—but generally invisible—actors in socioeconomic development. Men are more active in the formal sphere, where government-sponsored (and foreign-funded) development activities usually take place; women are more active in the informal sphere, which provides the economic base for the formal sphere.

Rural-Urban Equity

Many developing societies are characterized by **dualism**—a tiny (often urban) portion of the population is rich, a small middle class dominates business and government, and a huge (often rural) population lives at subsistence or even below survival levels.[22] Dualism is most obvious in

Women, seen here pounding grain in Jumla, Nepal, are key—but
generally invisible—actors in socioeconomic development. (Photo
by Melissa Yazman, courtesy of Winrock International)

large cities—Bombay, Buenos Aires, Cairo, Calcutta, Jakarta, Manila, Mexico City, Rio de Janeiro, and Sao Paolo—but it persists throughout the fabric of developing economies, characterized in rural areas by wealthy landlords or owner-operator farmers and landless laborers or tenant farmers.
Those who are already well-off, both urban dwellers and rural villagers,
are usually better positioned than their disadvantaged fellow citizens to
benefit from foreign assistance. Rural-urban disparities are illustrated (in
countries for which data are available) by the differences in access to services. Compared to their rural counterparts, urban residents have greater
access to health services in 44 of 49 countries, water in 85 of 94 countries,

sanitation in 66 of 80 countries, and child nutrition services in 34 of 34 countries.[23]

Ethnic Equity

Ethnic and racial variation in economic opportunity is more difficult to measure and document. India's caste system persists despite its illegal status; Kurds are persecuted in Iraq and Turkey; South Africa's apartheid system is changing slowly after years of internal and international protest. Even in developed industrial countries, such as the United States and the United Kingdom, race affects economic opportunity and access to education, health care, employment, and housing.

Pakistan provides another example of the uneven distribution of both development activities and the gains from development. Green Revolution technology, particularly high-yielding wheat, was promoted by donors in Punjab Province. Although this province was perhaps in the best position to take advantage of high-yielding seeds, it is also the home of Pakistan's most dominant ethnic group. Other provinces have resource-poor agricultural conditions (deserts and high, arid mountains) and are inhabited by less powerful ethnic groups. As a result, development funds were devoted to Punjab at the expense of other provinces.

Equity is difficult to achieve when one ethnic group exerts economic and political dominance. Pilipino, based on Tagalog, is the national language of the Philippines. Philippine politics are dominated by Tagalog speakers who live on Luzon Island, where most of the population lives and which has long received disproportionate benefits from development. People from other language groups, such as Cebuwano, feel that the political system discriminates against them. Muslims have been denied access to the federal political process; the Moro National Liberation Front was formed as a response to this. The March 1986 Freedom Constitution, which authorizes local autonomy for Muslim-dominated areas, has helped defuse the tension. Despite donor efforts to dispense development resources to other groups, the government continues to favor development in areas in which Tagalog groups dominate.[24]

In Nicaragua in 1990, following the electoral defeat of the Sandinistas, the Chamorro government attempted to integrate the former rebels (contras), who had been fighting the Sandinistas, by establishing "development poles" for them in the south and central regions of the country. These areas received 10 percent of a $300 million aid package from the United States as a political reward to the contras for their years of resistance to the Sandinista government.[25]

The economic dilemma was initially summarized in the question, What is development? It can also be symbolized by the question, Why and how does development occur?

FROM DEFINITIONS TO THEORY
(FROM WHAT TO WHY)

As we have stated, socioeconomic development includes both physical achievements and human resource development activities; links between these two components vary from country to country, and nowhere are they completely understood. Advances in these sectors build on each other synergistically, and cause-and-effect relationships are complex and difficult to discern and quantify. In the interplay of technical and social processes, catalytic relationships depend on cultural and historical factors, and these are never precisely duplicated from one situation to another. Rigorous models of socioeconomic development—which inform donors by describing processes and desired outcomes—are both impossible to verify with precision and difficult to approximate in project implementation.

Moreover, budget and human resource constraints usually limit a country's ability to develop all sectors simultaneously. Education and health and transport do not develop all at once even with massive infusions of development assistance. They depend on complex interactions among values, institutions, and people. Because the relations between the physical and human sectors are little understood, these constraints lead to difficult choices for development planners. Which factors and sectors should receive priority? How should physical infrastructure and human resource development be coordinated?

Economic Theories of Development

Many theories have been advanced to explain how countries improve their living standards and to justify and design foreign assistance. There are economic and sociological models, capitalist and socialist models. Economic theories focus on the production and distribution of goods and services, whereas sociological theories focus on individual and group relationships. Capitalist models focus on the market mechanism and individual action, and socialist models focus on egalitarian outcomes. Common to all of these theories are the quest for the key ingredients needed for development and the attempt to identify prescriptions countries can follow. In their simple forms, both kinds of theories are incomplete; in practice, neither has resulted in the utopian world their advocates predicted.

Among capitalist economic theories and models, the laissez-faire prescriptions of Adam Smith are perhaps the best known. Smith argued in 1776 (*An Inquiry into the Nature and Causes of the Wealth of Nations*) that individuals who pursue their own self-interest without government interference will be led "as if by an invisible hand" to produce those goods and services that are best for society's welfare.[26] He extended this logic to relations among nations, advocating freedom of trade among sovereign states through the development of absolute advantage rather than following policies that encourage economic self-sufficiency. The policy prescriptions that follow are simple: Set fair rules for the market and let it work. Designing fair rules in the face of historical inequities that have left market forces uneven is difficult.

An indicator that is widely used as a measure of economic health is the domestic savings rate. In 1960, in *The Stages of Economic Growth,* Walter Rostow identified five steps in a linear progression to development: the traditional society, the preconditions for takeoff into self-sustaining growth, the takeoff, the drive to maturity, and the age of high levels of mass consumption.[27] Rostow and others defined the takeoff as beginning when an economy is able to shift from consumption to savings and to save 15 to 20 percent of its GNP, which can then be devoted to productive investment.[28] This model has had a profound effect on foreign development assistance planning.

Israel has followed Rostow's model closely, with massive infusions of development aid and external financing. However, although more savings and investment may be necessary for economic growth, these alone are not sufficient; other institutional and attitudinal conditions are also important, and each society must invest its savings in productive activities appropriate to its own history and current condition. Inflation and debt service can also offset high savings rates and leave countries with little growth. For all developing countries for the period 1980–1989:

☐ The average annual growth rate of per capita GNP was less than 4 percent, and 56 countries had negative growth rates.
☐ Inflation averaged nearly 25 percent per year and was more than 50 percent in 10 African and Latin American countries.
☐ Average debt in 1989 was nearly half of GNP, and in 22 countries, debts exceeded GNP.
☐ Debt service averaged more than 23 percent of the value of exported goods and services in 1989.[29]

Other economists have identified the relative dominance of agriculture as the key variable in economic growth: As an economy develops, the share of its gross domestic product derived from agriculture declines, and the shares of industry and services increase.[30] However, although this is generally true, wide variations are found among countries, and a country with a low share of agriculture is not necessarily developed. China and India derive similar proportions (27 and 31 percent, respectively) of their GNPs from agriculture, but China's per capita real GDP ($2,656) is almost three times that of India ($910), even though their unadjusted per capita GNPs are similar ($350 and $340, respectively). Agriculture accounts for about 17 percent of the economies of both Zambia and Greece, yet Greece's per capita real GDP ($6,764) is nearly nine times that of Zambia ($767). Similarly, Botswana derives the same proportion of its GDP from agriculture (3 percent) as does the United States, yet U.S. per capita real income ($20,998) is nearly seven times that of Botswana ($3,180).[31]

The difficulty with identifying an economic (or any other) prescription for development is that such prescriptions can never be completely specified. Economic conditions are never precisely duplicated from one country to another; nor are the social, cultural, and political environments in which economic development occurs. The social and political contexts of development can significantly influence the direction and impact of changes in economic variables that are the focus of development assistance.

From an economic perspective, improvements in living standards (development) can occur in three ways: reaping the gains of comparative advantage through trade, improving the efficiency of production, and expanding the technology of production. A country can buy a better mousetrap (trade), make old mousetraps for less cost (improve efficiency), or invent new mousetraps (expand technology). To increase food production in a developing country, farmers can buy (or be given) improved (imported) seeds and fertilizers (perhaps through development assistance), improve the efficiency of production with local seed varieties, or develop new varieties (or composting techniques) themselves.

Many arguments against development assistance are based on the belief that sustainable economic growth and development occur through trade among countries. Governments have long tried to benefit from trade and have often encouraged private entrepreneurs in this direction. The history of efficiency gains is also long: In their own self-interest, individuals are motivated to improve productivity, either by improving current technologies or inventing new ones. Governments can alter individual perceptions of efficiency through tax and subsidy policies to encourage entrepreneurial activity and induce change. However, developing countries may need assistance to implement effective policies.

The trade-versus-aid discussion is partly a debate about the relative merits of these approaches. Countries need both trade and aid in order to develop: Trade reaps gains from a country's current (short-run) **comparative advantage** (a country's ability to produce a commodity at less cost than other countries can produce it) in producing goods or services, whereas foreign aid often involves investments to improve a country's potential (long-run) comparative advantage, either by improving production efficiency or expanding production technology.

Unfortunately, the comparative advantage of developing countries often lies in either raw materials or unskilled labor, both of which are becoming less important as science develops synthetic substitutes for raw materials and labor-saving machines to replace male and female laborers. (However, there are as yet no substitutes for healthy forests and clean water.) Cheap labor from developing countries still attracts foreign investment; although this may increase the welfare of those who obtain jobs (directly or indirectly), negative environmental and health consequences often ensue for the people as a whole if industries are not carefully regulated.

Another side of the trade-versus-aid debate is the impact on donor countries. In the United States, some people argue that aid (which increases the productive capacity of poor countries) will reduce markets for U.S. products. Others claim that aid (which increases incomes in poor countries) will lead to more demand for U.S. products.[32]

Although private inventors and entrepreneurs—often motivated by the prospect of personal gain—have significantly improved production efficiency and expanded production technology, only recently have massive public investments explicitly tried to alter technology to improve the quality of life for small landholding farmers. The most notable examples of these investments are the international research centers that are financed by the Consultative Group on International Agricultural Research (CGIAR) system.[33] In addition to creating new technology, adapting and transferring technologies and information to farmers is equally important in improving the efficiency of their activities and in reducing the risk and cost of using these technologies. Both technological change and improving human skills to use technology are essential for development.

Theories of Social Change

In contrast to purely economic theories, which focus on the structure of economies and on the goods and services provided by societies through production or trade, sociological theories focus on social change as the key elements in socioeconomic development. From a sociological viewpoint, the concept of development derives from **modernization** theory.[34] Other explanations for the existence of underdeveloped, developing, and developed societies come from **dependency** (a theory that explains the underdevelopment and poverty of poorer countries in terms of their dependence on richer countries) and **world systems** (a theory that examines the political, social, and economic interactions of three sets of state and nonstate actors [core, semiperiphery, and periphery] within the context of a world capitalist market) theories.[35] The modernization school is the oldest of these; economic theories of development generally rely on this school for explanations of social change as a result of technological ad-

Both technological change and improving human skills to use technology, such as these tractor motors, are essential for development. (Photo by Dr. Noor Ahmed, courtesy of Winrock International)

vance and increases in agricultural productivity. Modernization theory relies on an evolutionary perspective: Social change is unidirectional, society moves from primitive to advanced, progress is good, and change is incremental.

Perhaps the most influential socialist explanation of economic development is **Marxism,** the economic, political, and social theory based on the work of Karl Marx and Friedrich Engels.[36] Classical Marxists consider the state to be a reflection of the ruling class within the capitalist mode of production. The state is expected to wither away under the dictatorship of the proletariat once **capitalism** (the system of production and consumption based on competitive private markets for goods and services) is replaced with **socialism** (the system in which all resources are state owned and their allocation and utilization are determined by central planning authorities) through revolution. Contemporary Marxists consider the state to be the primary impediment to development. The state, as the instrument of the ruling classes, makes allegiances with other states and with elite commercial interests that perpetuate social and economic inequalities and that develop infrastructure and resources to serve these interests rather than the society as a whole.

Development assistance was extended by the former USSR and China to introduce or support the socialist model in developing countries. Except perhaps for Cuba, which was heavily subsidized by the USSR, to date there has been no successful example of the socialist model of economic development. The most notable examples of socialist economies have either combined features of capitalist systems with heavy taxation to support social services (such as Sweden) or have proved inefficient in producing goods and services for their citizens (the former USSR and China).

Conditions for Assistance

Common to most development theories is the concept that changes from the status quo are needed to advance countries more quickly along paths to development. These changes may involve increased investments in physical infrastructure or human resource development or improvements in the policy environments in which physical infrastructure and human resource development activities take place. Because poor countries are often unable (or unwilling) to make such investments or improvements without external financial assistance (or political pressure), the conditions for foreign development assistance are created.

The most effective and efficient roles for foreign aid as a catalyst in development are topics for continual debate, as reflected in the constantly changing emphases of foreign aid programs. Agriculture has moved from commodity programs focusing on increasing the productivity of single crops (the Green Revolution) to cropping systems (several crops) to crop-livestock systems and now to farming systems (which may include agroforestry). In other areas, the emphasis has shifted from infrastructure (roads and dams) to basic needs (subsistence food production, health and education services) and now to policy reform. Trade rather than aid is often advocated as the preferred way to assist middle-income and upper-income developing countries. In all areas, investing in the social overhead capital of individual and institutional abilities continues to be important.

Development aid also contributes to the stability of international economic relations. Receipt of aid by a developing country is a tacit acceptance of the international market and trade **regime** (a set of norms or rules of behavior, based on formal or informal agreements, that provide a basis for institutions, conventions, and groups to address international conduct on particular issues) and of the desirability of participating in it. Aid is frequently targeted to increase a developing country's capacity to compete effectively in this regime. Agricultural projects that focus on the production of cash crops for export (such as vegetables, fruit, cut flowers, coffee, rice, cocoa, coconuts, wheat, cotton, and jute) strengthen the ability of states to expand their export markets.

The presence of aid increases the perception of economic stability in a developing economy. Paradoxically, a country receiving development aid may appear stable to foreign investors as a result of this intervention in its economy, and foreign investment often increases as a result of development aid. Donors often encourage recipient countries to reform trade and investment regimes to promote participation in the world market and greater foreign investment in the private sector. Kenya, the Philippines, and Thailand have experienced growth in foreign private investment as a result of reforms encouraged by development donors.

Although the emphasis within development aid programs has shifted significantly, these programs have been based on an underlying economic paradigm that embodies the principles of efficiency and effectiveness. The paradigm is simple: Make key investments in an economy, and long-term benefits for the society will result. Decisions on the content of development programs are often made using this paradigm. The changing focus of development aid reflects the evolution of answers to several questions: Where should these investments be made? Where are they most efficient and effective in achieving desired outcomes? What time period is appropriate to assess benefits and costs?

For practical implementation, theoretical models must be translated into practical policies, programs, and projects. The next section addresses the question of how theories are related to the practice of economic development.

FROM THEORY TO PRACTICE
(FROM WHY TO HOW)

Development theory—like all theory—must be based on past experience. Although the similarities among countries provide the basis for theory, no country ever precisely duplicates the conditions of another. Like other social science theories, development theories cannot be verified with the same degree of certainty as physical science theories. What works in Honduras may not work in Costa Rica or Indonesia. However, development assistance planners need not reinvent the wheel for each new project.

Even if theory approximately mirrors reality, it is difficult to distinguish cause and effect, and thus the implications for practice may be unclear. Income equality often follows a U-shaped curve, with equality decreasing as a country first develops and then increasing later. However, few practitioners would argue that promoting inequality will lead to economic development and later to greater income equality; the U-shaped curve is a symptom of development, not its cause. Similar observations apply to other characteristics. A greater share of the service sector in an economy may be a sign of development but does not necessarily cause it; Mexico derives a slightly greater share (61 percent) of its GDP from services than Germany (59 percent), but few would argue that Mexico is the more developed country.[37]

Descriptive theory is elaborated in terms of quantities or indicators that may not be subject to direct manipulation, and cause-and-effect relationships, even if approximate, must be the basis for practical policy. There may be many ways to influence an indicator of socioeconomic development, but not all may be desirable. The problem lies with choosing one or two measures to represent change that may or may not have a broad base within a given population. For example, do income distribution measures omit people who subsist outside of the cash economy? This distinction may be important in countries such as Bangladesh; it is also evident when national income data are disaggregated by gender. Development is multidimensional and complicated. Focusing on single measures may have unintended undesirable results as well as intended desirable ones.

The relation between per capita income and the distribution of that income provides a good example of the dangers of focusing on a single indicator, even one as well-known as income. As a country develops and its income level rises, income distribution generally becomes more equal, even though in the short run this distribution may be less equal. Unfortunately, the short run may last a long time, and income inequality may become a permanent feature of a country's economy. Wide variations are found among countries, and the poorest people in a (relatively) rich country may be worse off than the poorest people in a (relatively) poor one. For example, in 1988 the poorest 20 percent of the population in Brazil ($2,160 per capita income) had average incomes of less than $260, whereas the poorest 20 percent of the population in Morocco ($830 per capita income) had average incomes of over $400.[38]

In practice, a definition of development, elaborated through concepts and theories, is embodied in aid projects. **Development aid projects** (donor-funded activities designed to improve the lives of poor people in recipient countries) can be categorized according to their method of approach and area of activity. Most projects pursue one (or more) of three broad strategies: technology development and transfer, human resource development, and policy improvement.

Some projects attempt to introduce improved technologies to solve production, processing, marketing, or transportation problems; other projects try to increase individuals' skills and strengthen the organizations in which they work; still others are designed to improve the policy environments within which individuals and institutions can apply technological solutions to development problems. Most projects implicitly or

TABLE 2.3   Development Aid Projects: Sectors and Methods

	Sector		
Method	Agriculture	Industry	Services
Technology	Green Revolution Cropping systems Crop-livestock systems Farming systems	Food processing Agribusiness Forest products	Transportation Communications Medicines Power
Human resource development	Agricultural extension Agricultural institutions Research systems	On-the-job training Technical training Research	Management skills Technical training
Policy improvement	Food price policy Input price policy Credit policy	Import regulations Export regulations Investment policy	Universal education Health care

explicitly attempt to modify the values of their intended beneficiaries, particularly their attitudes toward change and their roles in inducing change.

There are also three broad sectors in which projects are active: agriculture and natural resources, industry, and services. The agricultural sector includes activities devoted to producing, processing, and marketing food and fiber. The industrial sector includes activities related to producing and marketing nonfood commodities. The services sector includes important areas such as education, health, transportation, and communication. In each country, the lines between these sectors are often defined by ministerial or departmental jurisdictional boundaries, and they depend on both the country's resources and the individual skills of the ministers or secretaries who head these organizations.

Table 2.3 shows the matrix that results from using both dimensions to categorize development aid projects. These projects have been based on a variety of models of development, each emphasizing different cells or combinations of cells in the matrix. This matrix also illuminates the choices development planners and practitioners face, such as what to emphasize and how to do it.

As experience has been gained with various approaches to development, practitioners have focused on different cells of the matrix shown in Table 2.3. The past decades have seen donor funds for international development allocated in at least five different ways: sectoral development, integrated rural development, basic needs, sustainable development, and structural adjustment.

Sectoral development, which focuses on specific aspects of agriculture, industry, or services, was pursued on the basis that particular sectors led development or that foreign funds and expertise were best devoted to large physical infrastructure projects. Sectoral development projects focus on individual columns of the matrix and fall primarily within the first row. In agriculture, early projects were often based on the Green Revolution, later ones were based on crop-livestock systems, and farming systems are now the basis of many projects.

Donors later recognized that development must often proceed simultaneously in many sectors and thus will involve more than one column of the matrix. The response, **integrated rural development projects** (IRDPs), combined work in several sectors—such as agriculture, health, education, and income generation—simultaneously as a way to remedy the single-sector focus of earlier development efforts. Unfortunately, these projects often created new infrastructure that was unsustainable by local governments. Costly and comprehensive, these projects peaked in popularity in the mid-1970s.

IRDPs once included activities in 30 of Nepal's 75 districts. Evaluations of these projects indicated that productivity gains were limited to large landholders; delivery systems for agricultural inputs were monopolized by the wealthy; the scope for applying and using the training extended through these projects was limited; accounting of financial transactions and project implementation was poor; project activities relied on local government bureaucracies and undermined villagers' traditional self-reliance systems; and these systems were not effectively integrated into planning project activities.[39]

Although IRDPs continue to be implemented in developing countries (including Nepal) with varying degrees of success, the basic premises of IRDP design—empowering local people and understanding that single-sector development is inappropriate in most subsistence-level environments—remains viable. This understanding has slowly been incorporated into donor programs.

The central problems confronting IRDP activities remain their expense and linkages with local government institutions. One study suggests that some powerful lessons learned through IRDP implementation are finding favor with donors in project design:[40]

☐ IRDPs should utilize existing local leadership instead of creating new structures that may not be socially or historically sustainable.

☐ Accountability for project implementation should be broadly participatory and not merely the responsibility of a few people.

☐ The donor agency and project staff should practice an open management style that includes project beneficiaries; this will help ensure a wide base of participation and support.

☐ Existing institutions should not be bypassed to create new institutions.

☐ Projects should build local capacity to provide technical assistance services.

□ Sustainability is not an automatic by-product of project activities; it must be consciously planned and nurtured.

The focus on **basic needs** (needs essential for a healthy life) emerged during the 1970s following the realization that bureaucratically implemented development would not result in benefits to subsistence farm families, landless people, pastoralists, urban unemployed and semiemployed laborers, small-scale nonfarm entrepreneurs, craftspeople, and female-headed households, which comprise the bulk of the population in developing countries.[41] A **bottom-up** (participatory development that involves beneficiaries in the design and implementation of development activities) instead of a trickle-down approach was advocated by the International Labor Organization, USAID, and the World Bank. This approach focused development aid on providing people with the basic needs of food, clean water, clothing, shelter, primary education, and access to health care. Integrated rural development projects evolved into a popular model in which satisfying basic needs could be approached from several sectors at once.

Sustainable development (development that recognizes that donor funding is limited and that attempts must be made to ensure that local capability can continue development activities after donor funding ceases) has become fashionable as environmental consciousness in donor countries has increased. Rising Third World debt has also increased interest in sustainability as governments—prodded by donors and international financial institutions—are reluctant to increase debt levels. **Grants** (funds provided by donors without a commitment by the recipients to repay) instead of **loans** (funds that involve a commitment to repay) are now preferred for development assistance. Sustainable development suggests that long-run development requires not only that technology be sustainable but also that training people and building institutions are critical to maintaining progress. It also recognizes that with high population growth, little development can be sustainable for long.[42]

Structural adjustment programs focus on policy (the bottom row of Table 2.3). These programs were created by the International Monetary Fund (IMF) and the World Bank during the 1980s in response to the debt crisis in developing countries. Although both institutions had programs and special facilities to help with balance-of-payments problems, the magnitude of the difficulties faced by developing countries following the oil price increases of the 1970s demanded a more coherent and comprehensive response from the primary international financial institutions.[43]

The structural adjustment strategy addresses both macroeconomic and microeconomic policies, based on the belief that lack of attention to policy

The focus on basic needs emerged during the 1970s following the realization that bureaucratically implemented development would not result in benefits to subsistence farm families, such as this Nepalese family. (Photo by Melissa Yazman, courtesy of Winrock International)

has hindered development efforts. Its main goals are to improve macroeconomic policy environments to attract investment and to stimulate trade and individual incentives. This strategy assumes a level of internal sectoral linkages and cohesion within the affected national economies. Unfortunately, such linkages rarely exist in truly poor countries.

Macroeconomic projects, such as those defined through structural adjustment, and the reforms mandated by the IMF and the World Bank, often cut across all of the columns of the matrix. These reforms often include currency exchange rate alignments, balance-of-payments adjustments, and interest rate revisions. Privatization is now in favor with USAID because governments are usually not the most efficient engines of development, even though in some countries the government is the primary force behind development efforts. Semigovernment parastatal agencies formed in the 1960s and 1970s to organize production and distribution are now being disbanded in many developing countries.

These shifts in emphasis probably result from a combination of shifting priorities, not-yet-failed passing fads, and—more significant—learning from experience. Aid projects now often take a longer view and recognize that sustainability has several dimensions—technical, administrative, and political.

CONCLUSION

Development is complicated, and the role of foreign aid in promoting development is likewise complex. Efforts to define, measure, and prescribe development goals and activities will continue to evolve as world conditions change and more information becomes available. Income, health, and education are generally accepted as key components of development, but relations among these components must be assessed on a country-by-country basis in order to design and implement realistic development programs and to define appropriate roles for foreign aid.

Development aid has political as well as economic dimensions. When poor countries seek financial and technical assistance from rich countries to help them achieve their development goals, political considerations are present in—and sometimes dominate—both donor and recipient calculations. These considerations are the subject of Chapter 3.

THREE

The Political Dilemma:
Why Do Countries
Help Each Other Develop?

Living in Nepal provided ample time for reflection. I had time to read and think and keep a journal of my daily activities and thoughts. Why were Peace Corps volunteers in Nepal? Why was the United States funding the Peace Corps? Why was Nepal accepting Peace Corps volunteers? Who benefits from—and who bears the costs of—the Peace Corps?

As volunteers, my colleagues and I did not expect to change the world; I realized that at best I might make a small difference in the lives of a few villagers. Little did I realize how much difference these villagers would make in my own life. Had I not joined the Peace Corps, I might have become a lawyer or a domestic policy analyst; when I returned to graduate school, my goals were clearly set on a career in international development. Since being a Peace Corps volunteer, I have lived in developing countries more than I have lived in the United States.

I joined the Peace Corps to experience something new and different, to broaden my horizons, and to try to help poor people. My colleagues had similar reasons for joining, and some were more serious than others. I did not see myself as a player on an international political stage. My goals, insofar as I had made them explicit, were humanitarian.

The Peace Corps' official goals were also humanitarian: to help poor countries and to provide a cross-cultural education for energetic young people. Some Peace Corps founders believed it was in the long-term U.S. interest for a large group of U.S. citizens to be familiar with the diverse ways of the rest of the world. Former Peace Corps volunteers are now represented in USAID missions around the world and in the U.S. Congress; their first-hand knowledge of poor countries should help U.S. development assistance policy to be more sensitive to the conditions in these countries and thus more realistic and successful.

In the early 1970s, Nepal's government was a constitutional monarchy, and a one-party political system served the wishes of the monarch. This political system was repressive, with little concern for human rights; stories of police beatings were common, and the press was tightly controlled. As invited foreign guests, Peace Corps volunteers were advised to avoid becoming involved in politics, but it was impossible not to engage in political discussions. However, these discussions remained largely abstract, with many villagers viewing democracy as appropriate for other countries and not directly relevant to their own situation; only a few villagers felt democracy was also suited to village conditions.

As Peace Corps volunteers, our responsibility was to help improve village living conditions by playing a small role in increasing food production. However, the quality of life has many components; improving the lives of Nepalese villagers may involve changes in political systems as well as in food production. In fact, significant increases in food production may depend on political change that results in improved incentives for agricultural activities.

Although some PCVs may have wanted to change Nepal's political system, we were in no position to directly influence it. Our tales of democracy in the United States, cumulated over the years, may have made a small contribution to the revolution that reconfigured the government in 1990; but credit for that change must go to the Nepalis who were actively involved. In fact, by helping the one-party government provide services to poor villagers, the Peace Corps may have prolonged the viability of this repressive system.

In the village, I had to decide how to spend my time. I could focus on the wealthier landowning farmers, who were able to take risks with new technologies but who were also using their positions as landowners to exploit their poorer neighbors. Or I could try to understand the position of poorer farmers, who had little or no land and lived mostly from their earnings as laborers for the richer landlords. I could spend time with the better-educated farmers, who were able to understand the concept of change and their potential for taking an active role in implementing that change, or with less educated villagers, in the hope that I could change their fatalistic ideas.

The explicit humanitarian objective of the Peace Corps is to help people; however, the Peace Corps (like USAID) falls under the U.S. State Department, which is responsible for defining and pursuing the international political goals of the U.S. government. These political goals include promoting democracy and stability and improving alliances with friendly countries. These goals may not be mutually consistent: Should Nepal's friendly repressive government be indirectly supported by humanitarian aid programs, such as the Peace Corps? Or should the United States push for democratic reforms as a precondition for giving humanitarian aid?

Peace Corps volunteers were not posted in the more remote mountainous areas for security reasons. Except for travel on one road, foreigners were not allowed within 25 miles of the Nepal-China border. This may have resulted from Nepal's earlier experience with the Indian Army, which for a time was posted along the Nepal-China border as one condition of a Nepal-India treaty. This condition was deeply resented by Nepal, which felt India had usurped its sovereignty. From a humanitarian viewpoint, people in these remote villages need assistance and would likely benefit from the presence of energetic PCVs who are willing to work in far-flung villages that are shunned by government officials.

This Nepalese example illustrates the key political features of development aid: Humanitarian and political objectives sometimes conflict, economic and security concerns are intermingled, and sovereignty is an issue for recipient countries. Although each donor-

recipient relationship is unique (just as every bilateral relationship is influenced by its own particular history), this example illustrates the complex political environment in which development aid takes place.

Even small countries are involved in international politics, and bilateral economic development aid is influenced by international political relationships between donors and recipients. Both long-term state survival and citizen welfare can depend on international relations, and on the welfare of other states' citizens, as well as on domestic conditions.

The world system consists of more than 160 states. Like individuals, states have friends and enemies. Friendships among states are maintained through official diplomatic and trade relations, as well as through private business, cultural, and familial ties. In addition to **bilateral** (activities that involve two states) treaties, which promote security and economic relations, states collaborate for mutual gain through **multilateral** (activities that involve many states) alliances (see Table 3.1). These relationships are complex and change frequently.

MOTIVATIONS FOR DEVELOPMENT AID

Most people want to improve their own standard of living, and many are concerned about poverty and want to help the poor. Unfortunately, personal budgets limit individual abilities to achieve both selfish and altruistic objectives simultaneously, and difficult choices result. Is it more important to save money for one's children's college educations, help sick friends, or give money to shelters for the homeless?

Likewise, most states want to improve the welfare of their citizens, and many try to help other states as well, in order to achieve both political (selfish) and humanitarian (altruistic) objectives. National resources and budgets limit states' abilities to achieve all of these objectives, and states must make choices. These objectives—especially the political and humanitarian objectives of foreign aid—may conflict. Should a country improve its own public schools, strengthen the military in a friendly country, or provide child health care for a poor country? Which is more important, domestic or international welfare? When do these coincide?

Although countries face difficulties in setting domestic spending priorities, in foreign development aid these problems are compounded by issues of state survival, security, and sovereignty. Should aid be given to poor, democratic countries, such as Mexico or the Philippines, or to even poorer dictatorships, such as Zaire? Who should have priority, flood victims in Bangladesh or war refugees in Iraq? These added ethical dimensions—choosing between political and humanitarian goals and between

TABLE 3.1 Political and Economic Alliances

OECD	ASEAN	SAARC	SADCC	OPEC	SELA
Australia	Brunei	Bangladesh	Angola	Algeria	Argentina
Austria	Indonesia	Bhutan	Botswana	Ecuador	Barbados
Belgium	Malaysia	India	Lesotho	Gabon	Bolivia
Canada	Philippines	Maldives	Malawi	Indonesia	Brazil
Denmark	Singapore	Nepal	Mozambique	Iran	Chile
Finland	Thailand	Pakistan	Namibia	Iraq	Colombia
France		Sri Lanka	Swaziland	Kuwait	Costa Rica
Germany			Tanzania	Libya	Cuba
Greece			Zambia	Nigeria	Dominican Republic
Iceland			Zimbabwe	Qatar	Ecuador
Ireland				UAE	El Salvador
Italy				Venezuela	Grenada
Japan					Guatemala
Luxembourg					Guyana
Netherlands					Haiti
New Zealand					Honduras
Norway					Jamaica
Portugal					Mexico
Spain					Nicaragua
Sweden					Panama
Turkey					Paraguay
United Kingdom					Peru
United States					Surinam
					Trinidad and Tobago
					Uruguay
					Venezuela

Acronyms are as follows: OECD—Organization for Economic Cooperation and Development; ASEAN—Association of Southeast Asian Nations; SAARC—South Asian Association for Regional Cooperation; SADCC—Southern African Development Coordination Conference; OPEC—Organization of Petroleum Exporting Countries; and SELA—Sistema Economico Latinoamericana. Other important alliances include the North Atlantic Treaty Organization (NATO), the former Warsaw Pact, the European Economic Community (EEC), the British Commonwealth, the Organization of American States (OAS), the Nonaligned Movement (NAM), the Islamic Conference, and the United Nations (UN).

Source: Based on information from Arthur S. Banks, ed., *The Political Handbook of the World, 1991* (Binghamton, N.Y.: CSA Publications, 1991), 891–1062.

We now usually have sufficient food to feed everyone, but its distribution depends on both domestic and international politics. Here, Bangladeshi men harvest rice. (Photo by Dr. Noor Ahmed, courtesy of Winrock International)

domestic and foreign welfare—transform already difficult budget problems into international relations dilemmas.

Development aid recipients have their own security and sovereignty concerns, and they must weigh these against the benefits of receiving aid. In this chapter we address the motivations for giving and receiving bilateral, multilateral, and private-sector development aid. We focus on the question, Why do rich countries help poor countries develop?

Since World War I, sovereign states—interested in cooperation and competition for influence—have extended international development aid through bilateral and multilateral efforts such as country aid missions, UN agencies, and development banks. Extending development assistance is viewed as important in reducing instability among states and promoting peace and in addressing worldwide resource scarcity problems in the face of the ever-expanding global population.

Although progress has been made in the area of food production, ineffective and unequal food distribution still plagues much of the world's population. We now usually have sufficient food to feed everyone, but its distribution depends on both domestic and international politics. Similar problems face the provision of health care and access to education. A challenge for bilateral and multilateral state-funded development aid is to address these problems efficiently and equitably within the framework of an inefficient and unequal set of principles governing state sovereignty and diplomatic practices.

If efficient economic progress were the only goal of development aid, the problems faced by developing countries—population growth, environmental degradation, debt and balance-of-payments crises, urban poverty, hunger, stagnating food supplies, sluggish centralized economies,

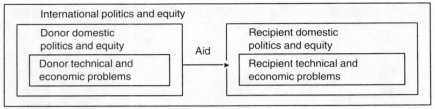

FIGURE 3.1 The international aid environment.

corruption, and inequities between men and women, between urban dwellers and rural villagers, and among ethnic groups and minorities—would be relatively simpler technical and economic problems complicated only by domestic politics and internal justice and equity issues. Because development aid is also extended for strategic purposes, these problems must be viewed from an international relations perspective, which adds another layer of complexity to an already complicated set of problems (see Fig. 3.1).

Traditional perspectives maintain that the first responsibility of a state is to maintain the status quo, both nationally and internationally—as long as its own interests are served. Other responsibilities include the provision of safety for its citizens and the designation of private and public property and of territorial borders. From these national security concerns, states seek to influence events and circumstances in other states. Motivations for foreign development aid often have humanitarian overtones, but much aid is given for two primary political purposes: Bilateral aid protects the national security interests of donor states; multilateral aid enhances the stability of the international system of states, thus increasing stability and security for all.

National security issues influence donor outlays for foreign aid activities, including humanitarian programs and disaster relief aid projects. Sustainable development efforts are difficult to maintain in the face of changing political priorities. Poverty has not disappeared despite billions of dollars spent on development, in part because this aid was distributed according to the political agenda of donor and recipient countries rather than the needs of poor villagers. Short-term concerns in the national security agenda of both donor and recipient states hinder the implementation of long-range development programs. The domestic political agenda of recipient states hinder the effective and equitable distribution of development resources, especially to the least advantaged citizens.

Critics of state-funded development claim that national political agenda make it difficult to stimulate long-term sustainable development directed toward the urban and rural poor. Others accept the political nature of development aid and focus on design and implementation issues, hoping to maximize the positive impact of an admittedly deficient mechanism. Although aid projects may be designed to benefit poor people, the politics of implementation may nullify these good intentions.[1]

Difficult political and economic choices face both donors and recipients of development aid. Donors must choose between funding domestic welfare and foreign aid, and they must balance development and security interests in allocating aid—particularly when donor and recipient priorities differ greatly. Recipients may feel they have little choice but to accept development aid, which may be designed by expatriates and presented on a "take-it-or-leave-it" basis.

Donor states continually engage in dialogue with their domestic constituents on the need to use tax revenues for development assistance. This dialogue is especially pronounced in the United States, Australia, and Canada, which have no history of colonizing poor countries. In the United States, aid must be justified in the face of declining funds for domestic social services. U.S. and Australian farmers criticize support for overseas agricultural development, claiming that increased output by foreign farmers may decrease their own export markets—even though income growth in poor countries may be the key to increasing U.S. farm exports.[2] The dialogue often influences development aid and has helped to justify subsidies for farmers from industrialized countries.

In contrast, several Scandinavian governments have development-oriented perspectives their constituents accept. These countries were the first to achieve the target agreed on by OECD members of providing 0.7 percent of national income as aid to developing countries (Sweden in 1974, the Netherlands in 1975, Norway in 1976, and Denmark in 1978).[3]

DEVELOPMENT AID ACTORS

The main organizational actors funding, implementing, and receiving development assistance can be categorized by their official status: sovereign states and their associated agencies, and nongovernmental (private) organizations. They can also be grouped according to their role in aid activities: Donors provide funds, implementors provide services, and recipients benefit from the funds and the services.

There are many sizes and forms of development actors: They include donor states, recipient states, foundation donors, nongovernmental implementing agencies, for-profit consulting firms, private village recipient organizations, and individuals. Table 3.2 indicates the variety of actors involved.

This matrix could be expanded to show the ways in which these actors are involved in political and humanitarian development aid projects. Donor countries could be identified according to their primary motivation:

TABLE 3.2 Categories of Development Actors

	Public	*Private*
Donors	States Multilateral agencies	Foundations Individuals
Implementors	Government agencies	PVOs, NGOs Consulting firms
Recipients	States	PVOs, NGOs Individuals

PVOs are private voluntary organizations; NGOs are nongovernmental organizations.

The United States, France, Britain, Germany, and the USSR (until 1991) would be on one side, with political considerations underlying most aid programs; countries such as Sweden or the Netherlands would be on the other side, with humanitarian purposes foremost; countries such as Japan, which has strong economic interests in providing aid, would be in the middle (these economic interests sometimes—but not always—coincide with the economic interests of recipients).

Many critics of foreign aid do not consider the complex incentives that motivate states, organizations, and individuals in their roles as donors, implementors, and recipients of development aid.[4] Little systematic analysis has been conducted on the motivations of the diverse actors and agenda involved in development assistance or of the effects of these motivations, actors, and agenda—in part because there are so many forms of aid. Identifying these motivations helps explain why countries give and receive aid.

Development assistance supported by public funds is provided through two types of programs: bilateral and multilateral. Bilateral development programs and budgets are influenced by:

- [ ] Political elites and public opinion in donor countries
- [ ] Concern for humanitarian relief and alleviation of poverty in countries that are important to donors
- [ ] The need for international economic and social stability
- [ ] Historical links between donors and recipients
- [ ] The importance of developing countries as economic partners (sources of labor and raw materials, markets for imports and exports)
- [ ] Security interests, strategic concerns, and regional responsibilities
- [ ] Political decisionmaking and budget processes in donor states

Multilateral development programs are influenced by:

- [ ] The need of donors and recipients for institutions to coordinate development efforts at the country, regional, and international levels

☐ The ability of multilateral agencies to initiate and maintain credible discussions with recipient states on sensitive domestic policy issues
☐ The need to analyze the accumulated lessons learned from the development process across political, geographical, sectoral, and agroecological systems
☐ The need for insulation from bilateral political and commercial concerns in development aid disbursement and implementation[5]

Politics affects the allocation of development aid in many ways. Strategic military concerns, economic stability, national security, domestic business, colonial history, human rights, power, and religion all influence the amounts of aid provided to recipient countries for particular programs. Bilateral aid programs are more obviously affected by domestic donor and recipient politics than is multilateral aid. **Multilateral development organizations** (which have many states as members) have their own political concerns and are often influenced by the security and economic concerns of their largest donors.[6]

Understanding state motivations is important because states—through bilateral and multilateral activities—fund most international development. Private sources fund commerical investments, foundations, **nongovernmental organizations** (NGOs) (typically nonprofit, nonofficial organizations that are actively involved in the process of socioeconomic development), and **private voluntary organizations** (PVOs) (organizations supported primarily by private donations and for which service, not profit, is the primary motivation). PVOs and NGOs work with poor communities at the local level, implementing projects that states cannot or will not carry out through bilateral or multilateral development programs. Despite increased funding from private sources, states remain the largest financial contributors to developing countries, providing nearly 60 percent of the more than $130 billion in annual resource flows to these countries.[7] **Official Development Assistance** (ODA) (flows from donor governments to recipient governments or multilateral organizations) accounts for more than $60 billion of these funds.

Although OECD members agreed in the 1960s to allocate 0.7 percent of GNP for Official Development Assistance, few countries have realized that goal. Among the 12 OECD donor countries providing more than $1 billion per year in aid, only Denmark, the Netherlands, Norway, and Sweden give more than 0.7 percent of their GNPs. France and Germany each provide more than $5 billion annually, but as a proportion of GNP their contributions are only 0.4 and 0.6 percent, respectively; Japan and the United States each provide more than $10 billion per year, but this is only 0.3 percent of each country's GNP. In contrast, Saudi Arabia and the UAE each give more than 2 percent of their GNPs in aid.[8] China and India pro-

vide relatively small amounts of assistance, but these funds can be important in the regions in which they are focused.

Of the 98 countries receiving ODA for which information is available
for 1990, 12 received more than $1 billion per year. The impact of this aid
varied widely among recipient countries:

□ In 55 countries, ODA was less than 10 percent of GNP.
□ In 20 countries, ODA was between 10 and 20 percent of GNP.
□ In 9 countries, ODA was more than 20 percent of GNP.
□ In 68 countries, ODA was less than $50 per capita.
□ In 23 countries, ODA was between $50 and $100 per capita.
□ In 7 countries, ODA is more than $100 per capita.[9]

There are many types and sizes of aid activities: Programs and projects
are funded by single donor countries, multiple donor countries, international agencies, humanitarian organizations, foundations, and even individuals. These activities may be implemented by public or private agencies, and the direct and indirect beneficiaries may be public or private
organizations or individuals. Although these categories are not mutually
exclusive, and purposes sometimes conflict or overlap, for analytic purposes development aid activities can be categorized according to the two
primary objectives—political and humanitarian—for which most aid is
given.

The development aid dilemma for donors is to choose between selfish
and altruistic motives in allocating state budgets. This involves making
choices between domestic welfare and development aid and between political and humanitarian goals. The dilemma for aid recipients is to choose
between the benefits of accepting aid and the loss of freedom that may accompany restrictions attached to aid. State motivations for providing and
receiving development assistance involve both security and economic
goals, which are reflected in aid provided for political or humanitarian
purposes.

As with donors, the motivations of recipient governments may be political or humanitarian. Recipient governments may want the benefits directly provided by development aid, or they may have more indirect political objectives. Aid may be used by recipient governments for
international political purposes, playing off donors that are competing for
influence. Governments may want funds to pay for social programs they
cannot initiate but for which they may eventually want to assume financial control. Aid may be used for domestic political purposes to reward
groups that support the regimes that are in power. Such rewards affect the
success of development activities, because more effective neutral organi-

zations may be passed over as implementing agencies in favor of politically supportive organizations.

POLITICALLY MOTIVATED AID

Examples of development aid given to achieve a political end (**politically motivated aid**) include a donor allocation that represents (implicitly or explicitly) the price of a vote on an international issue in the United Nations or that is provided as part of the rent for a military installation: The donor's motivation is unrelated to specific projects, and the donor's primary purpose of the aid is achieved when the donor itself has benefited. Politically motivated aid can be used to achieve humanitarian goals, but these are secondary. The outcomes of projects funded through such allocations are irrelevant to the donor, whose purpose may be to benefit implementing organizations in the donor country or to secure support for a particular policy position. In such situations, donors can easily overlook recipients' misuse of funds, because the benefit to the donor is more important than the effect on recipients.

Politically motivated aid is usually funded by national governments and is frequently implemented by private-sector organizations, such as local and expatriate consulting firms. Decisions on allocating politically motivated aid may be divorced from decisions regarding the substance of the economic development programs such aid finances. These programs are implemented by private-sector actors or PVOs/NGOs that may have little interest in states' political motivations. The political end is advanced by the provision of aid, not by the successful implementation of the activities it funds.

Political development aid is provided primarily by sovereign states: The United States gave development aid to the Philippines partially as payment for maintaining U.S. military bases there, and it reduced that aid when the Philippine Senate refused to renew the bases treaty; the United States reduced aid to Zimbabwe in 1984 because it disagreed with Zimbabwe's votes in the United Nations; the USSR provided aid to Cuba to maintain a foothold in the Western Hemisphere; France maintains strong economic relations with former colonies in West Africa, as does Britain with some Commonwealth countries. Politically motivated aid is usually tied to donors' foreign policy concerns and may be given for ideological purposes: The United States has provided aid to Latin America to discourage Communist governments and to protect long-standing U.S. commercial interests there.

Politically motivated aid is viewed by donors in the overall context of their foreign relations with recipient countries and other potentially affected countries. Donor countries frequently try to soften the impact of politically motivated aid and to create a humanitarian image through volunteer programs, such as the U.S. Peace Corps; the Dutch, British, Swedish, Japanese, and Canadian governments all have volunteer programs. Although volunteers' work is not explicitly tied to political objectives, it is indirectly linked through overall aid programs for specific countries. In the past, the U.S. Peace Corps has voluntarily left, or has been asked to leave, countries with whose governments the United States disagreed, such as India, Chile, Afghanistan, and Brazil.

Although international organizations are sometimes used as vehicles for humanitarian aid by states that maintain separate bilateral aid programs with more overtly political objectives, some official bilateral aid is also motivated by humanitarian concerns. Likewise, strings may be attached to humanitarian aid by politically motivated donors. USAID may give a PVO such as the Cooperative for American Relief Everywhere (CARE) a grant to use at its discretion, but CARE must reflect USAID concerns to obtain continued funding. Some PVOs, such as Oxfam (USA), have refused to apply for USAID grant funds because of this potential conflict of interest.

Politically motivated development aid often serves two concerns of donor states: strategic and economic. These are discussed in the next two sections.

Strategic Motivations

Politics has often influenced U.S. development aid to Pakistan. After a long history of supplying aid, in October 1990 the United States cut off economic and military aid worth nearly $600 million a year following renewed fears that Pakistan had developed nuclear weapons.[10] Congress invoked the 1985 Pressler Amendment to the Foreign Assistance Act (which Presidents Ronald Reagan and George Bush had previously waived), under which U.S. aid depends on certification that Pakistan does not possess an "explosive nuclear device." President Bush did not provide the required certification, so Congress stopped sending aid.

Although Pakistan and India signed a treaty in January 1991 pledging not to attack each other's nuclear installations, this did not assuage U.S. fears that Pakistan was developing nuclear weapons (to match those of India), which might be used in the long-festering territorial conflict over Jammu and Kashmir. However, following a May 1991 meeting of the Pakistan Aid Consortium, Pakistan and the United States resumed aid discussions. Although President Bush allocated military aid for Pakistan in the 1992 budget, Congress voted to retain strict conditions on economic and military aid. Congressional resolve was strengthened by China's confirmation that Pakistan had recently purchased short-range tactical missiles.[11]

Although Pakistan has been an important recipient of U.S. aid (particularly after the Soviets invaded Afghanistan in 1978), its ability to use this and aid from other donors effectively has been hampered by regional politics, corruption, and inefficiency. Pakistan's primary focus has been to strengthen its defense against India and protect its territorial claims; internal regime maintenance stands in second place, and socioeconomic development needs run a distant third. This emphasis on defense has come at the expense of social development. Despite a reduction in the number of people living in poverty, many social indicators have not improved. In 1990, life expectancy at birth was 58 years, and child (under 5 years) mortality was 162 per thousand. Adult literacy was only 43 percent for men and 18 percent for women.[12] Development aid to Pakistan—although improving agricultural and industrial production and providing infrastructure, such as roads, bridges, and irrigation—has not significantly improved the quality of life for most male or female Pakistanis.

U.S. development and military aid flows to Pakistan are unlikely to resume until an understanding is reached on nuclear weapons, even if other donors provide development aid to Pakistan. Given the long-standing disputes between Pakistan and India, the Jammu-Kashmir conflict is unlikely to be resolved quickly, and Pakistan will continue to have an interest in acquiring nuclear weapons. For Pakistan, the chances of receiving development aid to improve the lives of its poor people depend on its relations with donors, and these relations in turn continue to be influenced by its disputes with India.

The 1991 rejection of the U.S. military bases treaty by the Philippine Senate has profoundly affected the way the United States views the Philippines in relation to national security interests. Because the Philippines will no longer host U.S. military installations, the importance of assisting Philippine development efforts is diminished. Both parties now describe this relationship in economic rather than strategic terms, with an increased emphasis on trade rather than aid.

Future U.S. foreign aid outlays—economic support funds, military aid, and food and development aid—will reflect the Philippines' diminished strategic importance to the United States; in a two-year period (FY 1992 and FY 1993) aid has been reduced by three-quarters. In the long run this may be positive for the Philippines, but in the short run available development funds are reduced. Foreign and domestic investments may also decrease, because the U.S. military was viewed as a stabilizing force in a volatile political environment. Continued political stability will help restore investor confidence in a base-free Philippines, and Japan may increase development aid to the Philippines, thus partially offsetting U.S. reductions.[13]

Decisions about aid for Eastern Europe and the new countries that once comprised the Soviet Union are being made by the United States and Western Europe according to their desire and need for political stability in Eastern Europe. Stabilizing these floundering economies, thus reducing threats to national security within Europe, is of utmost sensitivity. Future control of the former Soviet nuclear arsenal will influence donor decisions. Development aid may help reduce long-repressed ethnic tensions that have resurfaced in part because of economic instability and shortages. This need is particularly acute in the former Soviet Union and Yugoslavia, but it is critical for other countries as well.

The United States and Western Europe have been accused of neo-imperialist and neocolonialist motivations in making development aid decisions. This accusation is difficult to verify. All donor countries tend to give aid to countries that are sympathetic to their national security concerns and with which they enjoy historical relationships, including former colonies or associated territories. Former Western European colonial powers maintain special relationships with former colonies, especially in Africa. France has concentrated its development aid over the past 20 years on its former colonies (primarily in Africa), and Britain has focused on members of the British Commonwealth (in Asia and Africa).[14]

Cold War competition between the USSR and the United States from 1945 to 1985 profoundly affected development aid allocations. The USSR focused most of its aid after World War II and the Korean War on Eastern Europe and North Korea, shifting later to Cuba, Viet Nam, and Mongolia; other developing countries received development aid if strategic competition existed with the United States (such countries include Afghanistan, Angola, Egypt, Ethiopia, India, Iraq, Mexico, Mozambique, Nepal, Nicaragua, Pakistan, Syria, and the Democratic Republic of Yemen).

Although Japan and the OPEC countries have different values and motivations for providing development assistance than those of the United States or Western Europe, they too give aid for national security reasons. Japan focuses on Asian countries and provides development aid that furthers Japanese commercial interests. Saudi Arabia gives aid to poorer Islamic countries to strengthen governments and enhance diplomatic relations.

Even when aid flows between two states remain constant, politics affects development programs. Recipients often criticize donor-driven development, feeling they have little influence over the design and implementation of such aid programs. This can be positive when donors pressure repressive governments to empower poor people or to improve the welfare of disadvantaged minorities. Many PVOs/NGOs and foundations funding projects in China and Myanmar view their presence in this context.

Cold War competition between the USSR and the United States from 1945 to 1985 profoundly affected development aid allocations to people such as these Vietnamese villagers. (Photo by Janet Sturgeon, courtesy of Winrock International)

Donors can also pressure recipient governments to accept ill-designed, politically motivated aid projects. The Coppice Reforestation Project in Nepal was motivated in part by the personal interest of a U.S. congressman who wanted to promote opportunities for friends in the tree seedling business. The project was originally designed to import millions (far more than could be used) of poplars (a fast-growing tree with limited use in Nepal's middle hills) at high cost (refrigerated air freight) for planting in Solukhumbu, a mountain district that is an inappropriate location for this tree.[15] This project failed because it was technically unsound. Had the species been appropriate for the region, the motivation for the project might have been irrelevant. Unfortunately, politically motivated projects frequently lack adequate technical planning to ensure success.

Development aid is a two-way street: Both willing recipients and willing donors are needed to formalize aid agreements. Although Nepal has agreed to accept all the foreign aid it has received, too often there has been a reluctance to refuse aid, even if it is inappropriate to Nepal's needs. Nepalese officials feel they are in a weak position vis-à-vis foreign donors, and

too many aid agreements are undoubtedly characterized by the phrase ut-
tered facetiously by a high official after signing a "joint" agreement: "Yes,
we both agree that this is what you [the foreign donor] want."[16] Nepal is
not unique; many poor countries find it politically and economically difficult to refuse offers of development assistance.

Economic Motivations

Domestic private-sector concerns also affect aid allocation procedures.
To promote U.S. business, USAID now requires all of its contractors to
purchase U.S.-made goods and vehicles for development projects. This requirement, which benefits U.S. business, is also used to help justify the development aid budget. For the development organizations implementing
USAID-funded projects, this is often a cumbersome, inefficient, and im-
practical requirement that delays project progress. Britain also ties its development aid to procurement of British goods, as do many other donors.
Nearly half of all bilateral aid provided by Development Assistance
Committe (DAC) members (which is three-fourths of their total aid) is tied
to procurement in the donor country. Japan ties less than one-fourth of its
bilateral aid to procurement of its goods, and the United States ties nearly
two-thirds of its aid to such procurement.[17]

Although socialist countries have provided some development assistance (sometimes to balance capitalist contributions), most development
aid flowing from industrialized countries to developing countries is extended within the context of the capitalist market and the Western development model. With the dissolution of socialist governments in Eastern
Europe and the former Soviet Union, the future of socialist aid rests with
China. Historically, Chinese development aid has supported friendly but
weak socialist states, such as Cambodia, Mozambique, and Tanzania, or
has bought influence in strategic areas, such as Nepal. Chinese aid has
also been given to counteract aid from the Soviet Union or India. Indian
aid has primarily gone to small neighboring states such as Bhutan, Sikkim
(prior to 1974), Nepal, and the Maldives.

How can development aid be targeted for long-term projects that require patience in funding and implementation if donors continually alter
their aid budgets with changes in domestic and international political
events? Fortunately, donors have long-term humanitarian objectives as
well as short-term political goals when decisions are made for providing
development aid.

HUMANITARIAN DEVELOPMENT AID

Development aid given to achieve humanitarian ends (**humanitarian
development aid**) can be illustrated by projects that provide training for

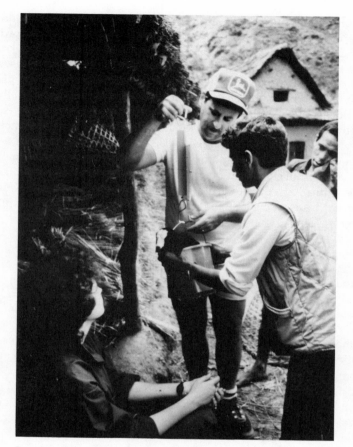

Development aid given to achieve humanitarian ends can be illustrated by projects that provide training for villagers in the hope that
they will gain useful skills. Training Nepalis to weigh goats is an example. (Photo by Melissa Yazman, courtesy of Winrock International)

villagers in the hope that they will gain useful skills and thus improve
their lives. In contrast to politically motivated aid, in which the end is a
benefit for the donor, here the end is a benefit for the recipient. The motivating philosophy is humanitarian—the purpose is to respond to recipient needs, not to donor politics.

Humanitarian development aid is provided by multilateral agencies,
bilateral government aid programs, and nongovernmental organizations
whose stated purposes are long-term economic development and social
change. For example, the UN International Children's Emergency Fund

(UNICEF) funds nutritional programs in Brazil; the United States provides aid for resource conservation projects in Nepal; and the Ford Foundation supports agricultural research in West Africa. Nongovernmental organizations that provide humanitarian aid include foundations, private voluntary organizations, charitable organizations, and religious groups.

Even though humanitarian aid is less ideological than politically motivated aid, its success often depends on friendly relations between nongovernmental implementors and host country government agencies. Private-sector development organizations must also interact with recipient states, even when private-sector activities are intended to benefit local nongovernmental organizations or individuals. For example, maintaining good relations with the government's Social Services National Coordination Council has been essential for private development organizations working in Nepal.

Enhancing national capacity to address developmental problems is a primary goal of much humanitarian development aid, which is frequently characterized by participatory strategies that stress grass-roots and people-centered activities. Bilateral and multilateral agencies, foundations, PVOs, and NGOs have spent billions of dollars toward this end. Much technical assistance is designed to increase the capability of host institutions and provide training to host country nationals.

Humanitarian aid is funded by both private and public sources. Implementation is sometimes carried out directly by the funding organizations and sometimes by private-sector actors. Decisions on the allocation of humanitarian aid by donors are usually directly related to national government decisions regarding the substance of development programs and projects, because the underlying goal of this aid is directly related to successful implementation and sustainability.

The Aga Khan Rural Support Program (AKRSP) may be the most successful example of externally funded integrated rural development. Funded primarily through the private Aga Khan Foundation, this project is located in a remote area of Pakistan inhabited mostly by Ismailis who view the Aga Khan as both a spiritual and a secular leader. The AKRSP is a carefully crafted program based on lessons learned from earlier attempts at integrated rural development and credit for the poor—these include the Comilla Project in Bangladesh (then East Pakistan) and the Daudzai Project in the Northwest Frontier Province of Pakistan. The program, administered by a charismatic, visionary leader, is based on community credit and local cofinancing. It has improved villagers' lives in northern Pakistan and helped build sustainable village-based institutions people trust. It has mobilized women for income-generating projects, literacy, skills development, and health care and—most important—helped them gain the confidence they previously lacked to initiate projects.

The success of the AKRSP is based on consistent funding, strong leadership and committed staff, a population that trusts the donor's motives, and a strategy based on community and individual empowerment. The AKRSP has been criticized as being irreplicable because of Ismailis' unique loyalty to the Aga Khan and the deep pockets of the Aga Khan Foundation. Perhaps another factor that cannot be duplicated is the absence of any effective preexisting administrative or traditional authority other than the Aga Khan. The possibility of replication is now being tested by USAID, which is assisting the Sarhad Rural Support Program in its attempt to reproduce the AKRSP model of community empowerment and participation in rural credit schemes in other areas of Pakistan.

THE HUMANITARIAN
AND POLITICAL NEXUS

Two types of humanitarian development assistance can be profoundly affected by political concerns: human rights programs and disaster relief efforts. These are discussed in the next two sections.

Human Rights

Concern for human rights and freedoms raises the issue of how states treat their citizens and other people living within their territories. Donor states sometimes stop development assistance when persistent human rights violations occur. In 1991, Denmark froze its contributions to the Kenyan Rural Development Fund (a Scandinavian aid fund for Kenya) after state auditors found widespread corruption and misuse of funds by Kenyan aid officials. Britain and other donors also suspended aid to Kenya at the same time because of widespread human rights abuses by the Moi government. Voters in democratic donor countries are understandably uncomfortable with supporting—through development assistance—governments that do not respect international standards of human freedoms.

Over the years, donors have intensified their interest in the domestic politics of developing countries, citing the protection of human rights as a criterion for development funding. Tireless NGOs, such as Helsinki Watch and Amnesty International, and patient private and state donors, such as the Ford Foundation, USAID, the Canadian International Development Agency (CIDA), and the British Overseas Development Authority, have urged recipient governments to loosen control of the press, allow opposition parties, and protect the rights of citizens who want greater political representation and state accountability. For example, in its development assistance funding, USAID focuses on four areas: democracy initiatives, family and development, business entrepreneurship, and the environment. The democracy and business entrepreneurship initiatives encourage projects that increase individual economic and political freedom.

Although this pressure may bring positive results in recipient countries, it can be interpreted as using donor state power to interfere with recipient state sovereignty. Cynics claim that human rights requirements for aid are piecemeal at best, are long overdue, and will not be seriously implemented—especially in countries with the worst human rights abuses. On the positive side, experience has demonstrated that aid is more effectively and efficiently delivered under political systems that have adequate citizen representation, that have standards for measuring government accountability, and that provide incentives for economic entrepreneurship.[18]

Some critics claim that bilateral and multilateral donors have ignored human rights abuses and lack of political representation and that in such circumstances aid can only help to perpetuate bad systems. Many examples can be found of donor development aid supporting repressive or unpopular regimes—those of Field Marshall Mobutu of Zaire, Shah Reza Pahlavi of Iran, General Anastasio Somoza of Nicaragua, and Ferdinand Marcos of the Philippines are a few of the more notorious cases.

Disaster Relief

Disaster relief aid is a type of humanitarian assistance that has primarily short-term goals, although it is usually directed not just toward relieving immediate distress but also toward rebuilding infrastructure. It is perhaps best illustrated by an operation funded by private donations: The motivation of the donors is to help unfortunate people affected by the disaster, and the operation's purpose—to benefit recipients by alleviating immediate hardship—is transparently the same for both donor and recipients. Donors want to help and to gain goodwill; recipients want help and in most cases remember the goodwill.

Disaster relief aid may be provided by either government or nongovernmental organizations: The United Nations High Commission for Refugees helps Cambodian refugees; the United States assists drought victims in Africa; and the International Red Cross provides assistance for earthquake victims. The immediate purpose of government-funded disaster aid is short-term alleviation of suffering, but its long-term purposes may be political as well as humanitarian. Both international and domestic politics can play significant roles in relief aid: The supply and distribution of food in Ethiopia in 1984–1986, and more recently in Somalia, were strongly influenced by external and internal politics. During the 1991 Gulf War, some states constrained the delivery of relief aid to Kurdish refugees in Turkey and Iraq; private organizations overcame state restraints to deliver relief aid effectively through UN agencies.

Like humanitarian aid, disaster relief is funded from both private and public sources, and implementation may be undertaken by the funding agencies or by other organizations. When political factors are important, decisions on disaster aid allocation may be divorced from decisions on implementation.

Because disasters may have political causes (such as war) as well as natural causes, political factors are often of overriding importance in both the allocation and implementation of relief aid; examples abound of politics delaying and preventing relief to refugees of civil or international wars, as occurred in the conflicts in Somalia, Ethiopia, and the former Yugoslavia. The combination of politics, large amounts of resources being delivered to relatively small numbers of people, and necessity for quick decisions also creates a great potential for corruption.

The cyclone that struck Bangladesh in April 1991 provides an illustration of these political factors. The cyclone hit the ports of Chittagong and Cox's Bazar, killed at least 139,000 people, destroyed water systems, and left thousands dying or seriously threatened by diarrheic epidemics. The area's lucrative shrimp industry was seriously damaged, 44 military planes were lost, and helicopters, naval ships, and harbor facilities were damaged. In mid-May, the Bangladesh government requested $670 million in disaster relief aid and an additional $740 million for reconstruction. Donors delayed because they were suspicious of the government's delay in assessing cyclone damage. Critics claimed the government was slow to respond for political reasons and because of bureaucratic malaise (resulting from incapacity, politics, low salaries, and low esteem) in the Bangladesh civil service.

On May 20, Bangladesh agreed to let a U.S. task force help coordinate government relief efforts. Because of the successful use of the U.S. military to help coordinate relief service to the Kurds in Iraq and Turkey, and as an example of the U.S. role in a "new world order," 400 U.S. Marines and construction workers with helicopters and amphibious landing ships were sent to Bangladesh. Opposition parties claimed U.S. military involvement in relief activities seriously threatened Bangladesh's national security. On May 30, the Bangladesh Aid Consortium (convened by the World Bank) announced it would increase long-term assistance to offset reconstruction costs.[19]

This example illustrates the controversial role played by military personnel in relief services and the potentially negative role domestic politics can play by delaying the damage assessment of a natural disaster. Innocent people suffered from this delay, and donors were reluctant at first to extend funds to Bangladesh. Only after the U.S. military began to coordinate relief efforts did donors provide additional funds for reconstruction.

Little development aid is either purely political or purely humanitarian, and many development programs contain elements of both. The purposes for which aid is allocated may not be those of the programs and projects on which the money is spent. Disaster relief may be politically motivated. Development aid may be allocated to a country for political reasons and used for humanitarian programs, or aid may be given for humanitarian reasons and used for political activities, or aid may simply be consumed by the process of distribution through various government departments. There are many levels of decisionmakers and bureaucrats between those who allocate development aid and those who ultimately receive it; there are often several organizations in both the donor and recipient governments through which funds pass (and diminish at each step) before reaching the intended beneficiaries.

THEORETICAL EXPLANATIONS

As was discussed above, the motives of development aid donors and recipients can be selfish or altruistic: Donors provide funds to achieve their own political goals or to achieve the humanitarian goal of improving the lives of the aid recipients; likewise, recipient states accept aid to achieve their own political goals or to improve the lives of the intended beneficiaries. In international relations, these motives have given rise to three theoretical traditions—realism, idealism, and neo-Marxism—that attempt to explain why states, international organizations, and private-sector organizations participate in international development.

Realism

Realism, currently the dominant theory in international relations, focuses on the operation of an international system composed of sovereign states.[20] Realist theorists have a Hobbesian view of human nature—to them it is imperfect and selfish. This view of human nature is reflected in the formation and behavior of states and the international system. **Neorealism** incorporates an economic dimension into the realist perspective.

According to realist theory, sovereign states are selfish and competitive; they have created an anarchic international system that allows them to pursue their individual goals with minimal challenges to their existence. The anarchic nature of the international system results in strong states emerging from competition with each other for greater power. Strong states—defined by military capability—can act as hegemons dominating certain regions or as partners in balances of power.

In the international system, sovereign states respect no power greater than themselves. The only rules that exist are those that help states satisfy their primary desires for regime maintenance and security. Protecting sovereignty is the most important need of states, and this need drives both domestic policies and international behavior.

Although sovereign states are not the only international actors, realists consider states to be the most important entities in the international system. Despite their differences, states are the most similar actors in that system, which makes formal relationships among states fairly predictable. By sanctioning rules, norms, and patterns for their behavior, states also tolerate the activities of nonstate actors in the international system.

For realists, the terms *rich* and *poor, developed* and *underdeveloped* are less meaningful than *strong* and *weak*. A country such as Japan may have little military capability, whereas a country such as India may have highly developed military power. Socioeconomic levels reflect the resources states have invested in expanding their economies and improving their citizens' welfare. Military arsenals reflect perceived threats to state sovereignty, and development is defined by a state's capacity to mobilize its own resources and translate them into the ability to wield power.

The relative priority developing countries give to social services and armaments is starkly illustrated by their education, health, and military expenditures. Although on average both developing and industrial countries devote similar proportions of their GNPs to military expenditures (4.4 and 4.9 percent, respectively), industrial countries allocate more to education (5.9 versus 3.6 percent) and health (8.3 versus 1.4 percent). Of the 100 countries for which data are available, in only one industrial country (Greece; complete information is not available for Israel and the former USSR) is the ratio of military expenditure to combined education and health expenditures more than 50 percent, whereas this ratio is more than 50 percent in 45 developing countries and more than 100 percent in 20 developing countries.[21]

Sovereignty is a key concept whose importance is frequently debated in the international relations literature. Sovereignty is defined by the ability of a state to control internal and external problems. The exercise of state sovereignty can itself limit state freedom, particularly if a state decides to seek help from other states; many states have experienced reduced freedom of action after they have received development aid. Development aid ties both donors and recipients to the international community, and both groups are careful to support the illusion of sovereignty in the interest of maintaining good diplomatic relations. The extent of this illusion may be significant in countries in which the ratio of ODA to GNP is high: In 20 developing countries this ratio is more than 20 percent, and in Mozambique it is more than 75 percent.[22] Without aid resources, however, sovereignty may be weakened through poverty and the resulting inability to control economic and social problems.

Although their sovereign status makes them similar, states are not uniform in capability. The current international system is maintained partly through inequalities—in size, national endowments, population, location, and history—among states. This inequality creates stability, because states know that their military capability ranks them within the international system, which is structured according to states' ability to wield power over each other. Some states are far more efficient and shrewd than others in using national and imported resources to maintain their sovereign status.

For most realists, development aid is a tool used by states to help maintain the status quo of the international system. For multilateral donors, its purpose is to provide stability; for bilateral donors, its purpose is to counter the influence of rivals or gain support for policies. Rich countries provide aid because doing so improves the donors' positions in the world economy. Poor countries accept aid because it increases the resources available to strengthen their economies and governments and thereby to protect their sovereignty.

Some realists argue that development aid creates dependence. Others, mindful of state motivations to give and receive aid, view development aid as fostering interdependence. Development aid *has* resulted in increased levels of contact and cooperation—and perhaps in reduced amounts of confrontation and conflict—among states with different histories, levels of development, and cultures. High degrees of economic interdependence among states make independent state action risky, so threats to refuse international aid are rare and are seldom carried out. Although interdependence limits sovereign action, development aid is one benefit of accepting this reduction in sovereignty.

According to the realist perspective, rich states help poor states if they conform to the norms and rules of international behavior set by the rich, powerful states. These rules provide stability for the international system. Developing countries, such as Mexico and Brazil—whose economic problems have threatened the stability of this system—have influenced the setting of new rules governing debt repayment, greater accountability of development aid expenditures, and communication among bilateral donors and multilateral aid organizations.

What do donors do when their objectives diverge from those of their recipients (and vice versa)? Aid may be accepted by a government but conditions for its acceptance or implementation not be fulfilled. Humanitarian aid may support corrupt regimes and inadvertently slow the process of political change by promoting economic development and thus increasing domestic satisfaction. Donors may find their principles compromised, yet they may believe the greatest hope for improvement lies in maintaining stable, loyal aid relationships. Some donors may voice dissatisfaction in the hope of motivating recipient change; other donors may decide that the loss of influence suffered when leaving a country is less costly than continuing an unsatisfactory aid program.

Sovereignty issues must be considered in order to understand the reasons developing countries accept the interference and influence over internal affairs that accompany aid. Following the logic of realism, developing countries seek development aid to enhance their sovereignty and increase resources. Recipient governments are jealous of their sovereign authority over the area under their jurisdiction; nevertheless, they often accept the domestic policy intervention most development aid entails. In some cases governments may use conditions attached to foreign aid as an excuse to implement unpleasant, but necessary, economic or political reforms.

If control over domestic decisionmaking is eroded in the process of project design and implementation, recipients may view this as part of the price of accepting aid. In the long run, sovereignty may be enhanced as states gain greater power through development resources. Development aid is often considered an instrument to protect or enhance sovereign rights; aid and expatriate expertise have strengthened state institutions in many countries, even though poverty may have increased.

Dissatisfied with explanations that focus on sovereignty and strategic explanations for state motivations, scholars working from the realist perspective have developed a new subfield of international relations known as **international political economy**. This subfield sees the interactions among states as motivated by more than concern over sovereignty and security. State interactions are viewed as complexes of political, strategic, and economic activities. The motivations for these activities cannot be separated but must be considered within the context of the global market and international organizations concerned with security and system stability.[23]

Development is more complex than is indicated by realist theory, which does not consider the motivations for development aid beyond the sovereign state. The motivations of multilateral development organizations, as stated in their charters, transcend the parochial interests of their member states. Although the perspective of international political economy introduces economic motivations entwined with security concerns, both realism and international political economy conceive of an international system composed of, and dominated by, states. States remain the primary actors in this system, and development issues are considered within the context of states and the institutions they create.

Nonstate actors significantly influence development, so analyzing only the behavior of states is insufficient. The world system and the development process are not structured entirely on the basis of military strength.

Development aid also has a moral basis that realism discounts; this broader perspective is included in the idealist tradition.

Idealism

Idealism, another prominent theory in international relations, shares many realist assumptions about the nature and structure of the international system of states.[24] However, idealists discount power and sovereignty as the primary motivation of states and believe states can and do seek more noble goals than merely protecting their sovereignty through independent action; sovereign states have learned, through war and peace, that common problems can be solved collectively without significantly reducing sovereignty.

Idealists believe that states have many motivations, including the pursuit of power, and that humanitarian concerns are as important as sovereignty and security. Idealism contains the most plausible explanation of the complex motivations underlying the extension of development assistance from rich to poor states across cultures and history. Unfortunately, differences between idealism and realism have often been compared to the differences between speculative metaphysics and pragmatic policy.[25]

The idealist tradition views international law as the most effective means for maintaining order among states and holds that the anarchy of the international system described by realists can be reformed or restructured by the acceptance and use of international law. This law offers a practical (if imperfect) consensus for state action during crises, as well as rules and norms for acceptable state behavior. International laws and rules structure states' creation of multilateral development organizations, such as the UN Development Programme, the International Monetary Fund, the World Bank, and the regional development banks, which conduct their activities according to these rules.

Multilateral organizations are created by states for specific functional purposes and to help foster stability and order in the world system. Whereas realism focuses on the structure of the international system and the interactions of individual states, idealism focuses on the global system as it is managed by cooperating states. Multilateral organizations evolved in Europe in the nineteenth century as a means to help neighboring states resolve crises related to the use of common property resources. Their function is to foster peace and develop equity in the international system.

Collective action is considered the most effective means of transcending parochial state concerns. First embodied in global organizations in the twentieth century with the League of Nations, idealist principles of collective action and international law paved the way for the UN system and other international and regional organizations to maintain peace and foster economic growth. Collective action in development assistance can be seen in donor coordination and international relief efforts.

Idealist principles provide a paradigm for many development professionals, who are seldom motivated by realist sentiments. Most people working in development have humanitarian goals they pursue by working in donor agencies, private consulting firms, or PVOs/NGOs. These individuals believe in international cooperation and want to share skills and resources with developing countries.

Rich states provide development aid because they can afford it. Poor countries accept development aid because they need it. Development assistance benefits both donors and recipients because it promotes international stability and, therefore, greater opportunities for economic growth and prosperity. Although realist arguments can be used by donor policymakers and politicians to justify bilateral development assistance, idealist tenets are used to justify the activities of multilateral development organizations, foundations, and PVOs/NGOs. Idealists believe progress is good and that it can be achieved through state action. Poor people's lives can be improved by transcending narrow state concerns, replacing them with global goals.

Idealists do not ignore the pursuit of state power but see it in the context of other factors. What geopolitical advantage does the United States gain from providing development assistance to Nepal and Bangladesh? Aid to these states marginally counters Indian influence, but it has not significantly affected either state's relationship with India. Similarly, what security advantage will the United States gain from extending aid to extremely poor African countries? Idealists recognize the political and security concerns of donor states but do not view these concerns as the only determinants of interstate relations. Similarly, multilateral organizations are seen as functional organizations in helping states build a global community.

Two world wars convinced most states that it is safer to develop interdependence through functionally oriented multilateral organizations rather than bilaterally. When states realize that problems can be solved and mutual benefits achieved at minimum cost by reducing their individual autonomy, they usually agree to norms and principles that reduce this autonomy.

Multilateral development organizations comprise member states that join and contribute resources because they seek solutions to global problems through collective action. These organizations may be politicized, reflecting the agenda of member states. They develop their own values, norms, and procedures, which may conflict with the individual interests of member states. This set of rules, or regime, for international develop-

TABLE 3.3   Multilateral Development Organizations

Regional	Global
African Development Bank	Organization for Economic Cooperation
Asian Development Bank	and Development
Caribbean Development Bank	United Nations
Central American Bank for Economic	Economic and Social Council
Integration	Food and Agriculture Organization
Central African States Development	International Fund for Agricultural
Bank	Development
East African Development Bank	UN Development Programme
European Bank for Reconstruction and	UN Environment Programme
Development	UN International Children's
European Economic Community	Emergency Fund
European Development Fund for	World Food Programme
Overseas Countries and	World Health Organization
Territories	World Bank
European Investment Bank	International Bank for Reconstruction
Inter-American Development Bank	and Development
Islamic Development Bank	International Development Association
Organization for European Economic	International Finance Corporation
Cooperation	International Monetary Fund
West African Development Bank	

Source: Based on information from Arthur S. Banks, ed., *The Political Handbook of the World,
1991* (Binghamton, N.Y.: CSA Publications, 1991), 891–1062.

ment provides a structure for transferring bilateral and multilateral resources to developing countries.

Multilateral development organizations usually address international problems identified by sovereign states, such as the deteriorating environment (United Nations Environment Programme), widespread disease (World Health Organization), children's welfare (United Nations International Children's Emergency Fund), and the need for economic stability (European Community) (see Table 3.3). These organizations address issues that require maximum cooperation among states. IMF and World Bank structural adjustment programs require a tremendous degree of acquiescence from recipient states, and programs to reduce environmental devastation require significant short-term sacrifices by cooperating states. UN agencies and related organizations coordinate and lead state activities on these fronts. The Development Assistance Committee of the Organization for Economic Cooperation and Development records and analyzes flows of concessional development resources and facilitates communication among multilateral and bilateral donor development organizations.

Multilateral organizations derive their rationale from concerns for a stable international system and the common future of humanity. These organizations are based on the premises that states can cooperate and that nationalism can be transformed into a positive sentiment that supports transnational and international efforts. The United Nations is (and the League of Nations was) based on this paradigm, as is the European Economic Community. Designers of these organizations believed multilateral agency personnel would eventually transfer their loyalties from their home states to more global concerns.[26]

Globalism (a perspective that views all state and nonstate actors as part of an overarching system of political, economic, and social interactions) and **pluralism** (a persective that focuses on the diversity of state and nonstate actors within the world political system) have arisen as variations of idealism as analysts have attempted to view states as part of a global—rather than merely an international—system.[27] Scholars concerned with the influence of states, private commercial interests, global classes, ethnic groups, markets, religion, and gender on development view international relations from a **world political economy** perspective.

World political economy theorists view distributive justice as the moral basis for rich states helping poor states; the key issue is *how* the rich can help the poor, not whether they should. This perspective considers all development actors and seeks to explain the unequal distribution of wealth, the need for social justice, and the anarchic behavior that leads to war. The moral implications of these situations are reflected in state development assistance flows and regulations on commercial activity.[28]

World political economists try to map the behavior of states and of nonstate actors, as well as global trends that influence the basis of ethical behavior and the welfare of individual states. The interactions of the diverse actors comprise a global system that has its own logic for the distribution of wealth. The central organizing principle may be the capitalist world market, but the structure of the global system is also influenced by other forces, such as gender, class, and ethnicity.[29]

Neo-Marxism

Neo-Marxism, the third major theoretical tradition that tries to explain the underlying motivations for foreign development assistance, has several variants that explain how rich and poor countries have developed and the motivations for giving and receiving development assistance.[30] Neo-Marxism arose as a reaction to, and critique of, both idealism and realism; many of its contributors are from the Third World. This theoretical tradition views the motivation of states in the context of capitalist economics in which both states and the international system are institutional and conceptual results of the capitalist mode of production.

Neo-Marxist theorists concerned with gross economic inequities within and among states believe economic relations are more important than military power in structuring the international system. Considering the world capitalist economy to be the dominant system, with states as one group among many actors, these theorists see the flows of goods—among markets, states, commercial entrepreneurs, and regions—as indicators of the distribution of power. This paradigm attributes donor motivation to furthering the interests of entrepreneurs who control state institutions.

The organizing principle in the international system is the inequality created by international capitalism, which places states in three categories based on their capability for capitalistic production and marketing. The industrial core, the semi-industrial semiperiphery, and the agricultural periphery reflect uneven development patterns among states.

Capitalist production creates a market system based on a disproportionate distribution of wealth. Although countries lack equal factor endowments (land, labor, and capital), geography, or climate, neo-Marxist theorists maintain that the uneven distribution of capabilities among countries becomes a structural condition when economies are overly influenced by the world capitalist market created by industrialized countries. This first occurred through imperial and colonial relationships between European states and nations in Africa, Asia, and the Americas.

Neo-Marxists view development aid as tying the development of productive resources to international capital and the needs of core elites rather than to the needs of citizens (including disenfranchised or disadvantaged minorities). The state is then a slave to these external interests rather than the servant of its people.

In their efforts to understand the origins of world capitalism in the context of current global economic disparities, neo-Marxist scholars particularly concerned with the persistence of poverty in both developed and underdeveloped countries have devised dependency theory and world systems theory. These theoretical efforts hold that underdevelopment is part of the framework of the capitalist world market rather than the result of policy choices made by states. Development aid is an instrument of control used by industrialized countries to ensure that economic development in the Third World benefits their own economies and enhances their position in the international division of labor. Industrialized countries need underdeveloped countries to exploit, and development aid is a tool to help underdeveloped countries while at the same time keeping them poor.

Dependency theory arose as a critique of the UN Economic Commission for Latin America (ECLA) development model, which stressed trade protectionism and import substitution to stimulate economic growth.[31] Despite an initial period of growth, this model failed to produce sustainable growth in the Latin American countries that adopted it. Dependency theory has a socialist perspective and is supportive of Chinese-style and Cuban-style revolutions in which a peasant society does not have to experience a bourgeois stage before socialist revolution can occur.

Dependency theorists view Latin American impoverishment as being reinforced by political coercion, foreign investment, and foreign aid. National development efforts in social welfare and sectoral development are difficult for these countries because they are constricted by international corporate interests and indigenous elites with hierarchical values acquired from Spanish and Portuguese colonialism and the Catholic church. The interests that influence the locations of the means of production, circulation of advanced technology, and labor and capital flows in the international economy lead to the dependence of developing countries on industrialized countries.

The dependency model divides the world into the center (industrialized Western states) and the periphery (former colonies and poor countries of the Third World).[32] The periphery is underdeveloped because it has historically been exploited by Western Europe and the United States. Colonialism and imperialism destroyed the advanced cultures and productive economies that once existed in poor countries, interfering with each country's unique process of development. Developing countries are entangled in intractable exploitative relationships with industrialized countries that help industrialized countries to progress at the expense of developing countries. The only way Third World countries can pursue independent development is to sever ties with industrialized states through socialist revolution. During the late 1960s and 1970s, this path was pursued by several African countries, including Tanzania, Mozambique, Angola, and Ghana.

World systems theory arose from frustration with dependency theory, which could not explain why some Third World states were more advanced than others nor why some pursued relatively independent and autonomous development without undue influence from their colonizing countries. In world systems theory, which is based on socialism, the motivation of states for providing or receiving development aid is derived from the structure of the world market.[33]

The world economy, which has been largely capitalist since the mid-1600s, is a dynamic and fluid system. It is divided into three stages of development: the core (advanced industrial capitalist states), the semiperiphery (the newly industrializing countries [NICs], Eastern Europe, and the former USSR), and the periphery (the Third World). The semiperiphery contains elements of both the core and the periphery; it is the dynamic element of world systems theory.

Through the overwhelming degree of stewardship assumed by industrialized countries in regulating the international economy (through voting power and financial contributions to the IMF, the International Bank for Reconstruction and Development [IBRD], and the General Agreement on Tariffs and Trade [GATT]), the dependency of poor countries on development aid became a perpetual condition. The international division of labor is maintained through multilateral regulation of the world market and exchange rates, as well as by political and military influence over the commercial policies of poor countries. In this situation, poor countries will never be able to eliminate their dependency on foreign aid.

Several important distinctions exist between dependency theory and world systems theory. World systems theory uses the entire world—all countries and territories—as its unit of analysis, whereas in dependency theory the unit is the state. World systems theory has a distinctive approach (world systems methodology) that specifically adopts a historical perspective, and it rejects the determinism of dependency theory. Reality is considered a fluid process in which social entities, such as states, move into and through relationships with one another based on the current dominant mode of production and division of labor.

Neo-Marxist perspectives have contributed to the understanding of economic and social inequities within and among states. These perspectives have helped focus awareness on the effects of past and present economic relations, on inequities in the international trade regime, and on the overt influence of donor-driven development agenda on recipient countries' economies and cultures. However, neo-Marxist theory has not adequately explained dramatic changes in the international system, such as the economic growth experienced in East Asia (Taiwan, Singapore, South Korea, and Hong Kong), the significant changes among former socialist states (the Sino-Soviet split, the failure of the Chinese Cultural Revolution, the economic stagnation and crises of socialist states), the opening of socialist economies to Western financial institutions (the IMF, the World Bank, and private investors), the 1989 Eastern European democratic revolutions, and the dissolution of the Soviet Union. This failure highlights the inability of neo-Marxism to explain the motivation behind state-funded development as something other than a response to capitalism.

These three theoretical traditions—realism, idealism, and neo-Marxism—focus primarily on the motivations of state actors in foreign development assistance. Despite the new emphasis on world political economy and world systems theory, which give more attention to nonstate actors than to international political economy, none of these traditions systematically addresses the role of nonstate actors in development assistance. Although plausible explanations for the behavior of private-sector organizations can be drawn from idealism and neorealism, it is useful to examine these important development actors separately.

PRIVATE-SECTOR MOTIVATIONS

Private-sector aid is also extended for humanitarian purposes. In addition to efforts supported directly by private funds, sovereign states and international organizations sometimes rely on private-sector organizations to implement projects that would be difficult for public agencies to carry out at the local level. There are three main categories of private-sector development organizations: foundations, PVOs and NGOs, mercenaries.

Foundations

Nongovernmental donors provide funds primarily for humanitarian and disaster relief purposes. Major U.S. private philanthropic foundations include the Ford Foundation, the Rockefeller Brothers' Fund, the MacArthur Foundation, and the Pew Charitable Trusts. The Aga Khan Foundation is a well-known international foundation. These foundations are funded by private fortunes and often limit project or research grants to specific topics. Foundation-funded grants are often given to initiate discussions of important issues, with states or other donors funding further activities.

Foundations have played pivotal roles in human resource development and have been instrumental in providing both initial and continued funding for the international research and development institutions of the Consultative Group on International Agricultural Research. These institutions—notably, the International Rice Research Institute (IRRI) in the Philippines and the Centro Internacional de Mejoramiento de Maíz y Trigo (CIMMYT) in Mexico—have pioneered the development of high-yielding crops (rice, wheat, and maize) that formed the foundation for the Green Revolution.

PVOs/NGOs

The most prominent private-sector development actors are private voluntary organizations and nongovernmental organizations that depend on voluntary contributions. PVOs are primarily U.S.-based nonprofit organizations; in other countries, similar organizations are called NGOs, and in Africa, these organizations are called voluntary development organizations (VDOs). The numbers of NGOs in most developing countries have grown significantly in the past 20 years, and these local organizations are sought increasingly as partners by donors and expatriate PVOs/NGOs.

The motivations of PVOs and NGOs are primarily humanitarian. These organizations do not usually work in development to further the national interests of their home states, so they do not fit realist explanations of state-based development organizations. They may form organizations to help them work with governments (for example, lobbying groups such as Private Agencies Cooperating Together [PACT] and INTERACTION), but they do not look to governments for direction or guidance.

NGOs have a rich history that stems from the sixteenth century when missionary societies joined voyages of discovery and colonization. The International Red Cross Society was founded in the late 1850s to help the wounded during wartime, and national Red Cross and Red Crescent societies emerged later in individual countries. Most European NGOs and U.S.-based PVOs arose during the twentieth century in response to socioeconomic conditions created by the world wars.

PVOs and NGOs are formed by concerned citizens to do what governments cannot or will not do to help people in distress or danger (such as refugees). After World War II, colonial governments lifted many restrictions that had inhibited development activities by private nonreligious organizations. This liberalization—and the independence of most African and Latin American colonies—helped broaden the scope of PVO/NGO activities. Most development-oriented PVOs/NGOs now provide technical assistance, training, supplies, and organizational skills to improve village living conditions.[34]

Throughout their history, PVOs and NGOs have gained reputations for being in touch with local conditions in villages and rural areas and for having operational structures conducive to success at the local level. Because these organizations have humanitarian objectives and do not formally represent foreign or domestic governments, they are often the best vehicles for fostering local socioeconomic development. Bilateral and multilateral donors recognize the value of collaborating with PVOs/NGOs when projects need the participation of people in order to be successful. They are seen as operating independently of the foreign policy objectives of their home governments, even though they often receive grants from their governments' official development assistance agencies.

Expatriate PVOs/NGOs are important development project implementors, often acting as intermediaries between donor and recipient government agencies. Because they are flexible, humanitarian-oriented organizations, they often gain the trust of both national NGOs and local people. Their small-scale operation and focus on appropriate technology make them cost-effective, and their emphasis on participation by project beneficiaries throughout implementation helps make them successful.

Most religious organizations—such as United Mission, World Neighbors, Mennonite Central Committee, Catholic Relief Services, and Heifer Project International—that raise funds for development purposes concentrate on the secular aspects of their work, not on religious conversion. Their purposes are humanitarian; spiritual activities are usually focused on organization staff rather than on the beneficiaries of development projects.

The focus of PVO/NGO activity is to help the poorest segments of society (in developing countries, this can include much of the population). These organizations are generally not involved in infrastructural or market-oriented development projects, and their development perspectives often differ greatly from those of bilateral or multilateral development organizations that stress security and stability. PVOs/NGOs generally view poverty as caused by imbalances in wealth between rich minorities and poor majorities, urban and rural dwellers, men and women, or strong and weak ethnic groups. Part of the motivation of many PVOs/NGOs is to change these imbalances through direct action at the grass-roots level. Indirectly, some organizations try to influence unequal trade relations between developed and developing countries, international investment practices, arms sales, and the amount and mode of bilateral development aid.

NGOs/PVOs receive funds from voluntary contributions and do not rely on the consensus of tax-paying citizens for continued support. They can use more imaginative and flexible mechanisms to deliver goods and services than can governments, which gives them greater credibility among poor people. The more money NGOs/PVOs receive from voluntary donations, the more freedom they have; the more they rely on state funds, the less they are free to develop programs that are unconstrained by official preferences.[35]

International PVOs/NGOs are sometimes criticized for competing with recipient government services, for replicating or bypassing local agencies instead of pioneering new ways to improve service delivery within existing systems. Although government systems may be corrupt or ineffective, they are likely to survive longer than those developed and funded by expatriate organizations. International PVOs/NGOs counter this criticism by working with national NGOs and involving beneficiaries in all project activities.

PVOs/NGOs provide privately supported humanitarian development assistance to developing countries and victims of ecological or human disasters. However, they also want to gain influence and prestige in their home countries and in the countries in which they work, and they must generate contributions for further activities. PVOs and NGOs can also play political roles in the administration and direction of development aid; they lobby for increased development assistance funding and to promote allocations for particular programs.[36]

Donor governments frequently use grants to PVOs and NGOs to achieve objectives that are politically sensitive or beyond the scope of official aid programs. For example, USAID gives money to U.S. PVOs for population programs and family planning, which the United States may not want to appear to support directly.[37]

The fate of U.S. PVOs has been influenced by USAID's development efforts. Congress reacted to the failure of earlier USAID initiatives—such as Project Camelot and the Alliance for Progress—in Latin America, and the disclosure of Central Intelligence Agency (CIA) activities in Southeast

Asia and Latin America, by passing Title 9 of the Foreign Assistance Act of 1967. This amendment dramatically expanded USAID's grant funding for PVO activities to increase popular participation in, and acceptance of, development projects in recipient countries. In 1973, support for PVOs was strengthened with additional amendments to the Foreign Assistance Act. These amendments identified PVOs as the most effective channels for U.S. foreign assistance. Congress stipulated that grants to PVOs should not dilute the missions of PVOs but should help them expand their overseas activities. Despite this mandate, support for PVOs remains a small portion of the USAID budget.[38]

Mercenaries

Mercenary development actors are private-sector organizations that implement development projects.[39] These businesses sometimes compete with PVOs/NGOs for contracts to implement donor-supported development projects. Falling between donors and recipients, mercenaries have their own motives. Mercenary organizations, such as consulting firms and equipment suppliers, may implement both political and humanitarian aid projects if these fall within their areas of technical expertise.

Mercenary motivations include making a profit, but most organizations have the stated purpose of earning a profit while helping poor people. Development professionals frequently circulate among public, nonprofit, and for-profit organizations, carrying lessons and ideas with them. Although mercenary development organizations operate for profit, their employees often promote the perspectives and values of nonprofit and public organizations.

Private-sector development actors work in an environment dominated by donor preferences and recipient political pressures. Foundations and PVOs/NGOs have greater freedom than mercenary organizations because their financing comes primarily from contributions and grants rather than from donor-funded contracts. Mercenaries often serve two clients, implementing donor-funded contracts to provide services to recipients. To secure additional business, mercenaries must satisfy both donors and recipients, so good technical performance and good relations with both clients are important for success.

Private-sector development actors—PVOs/NGOs and mercenary organizations—must respond to conditions set by host governments at all stages and levels of activity, from overall development agenda to specific implementation regulations (such as procuring equipment, hiring local staff, and obtaining approval for specific activities). Because often their primary goal is to obtain business, with humanitarian objectives in second place, some consulting firms conform easily to donor project requirements. This is one of the primary distinctions between mercenary organizations and more ideologically motivated PVOs/NGOs.

Local NGOs are often created to provide goods and services to the disadvantaged or to perform public services (such as protecting the environment) when national governments fail at the local level. These NGOs usually lack substantial local financial support and are eager to accept assistance from expatriate donors, PVOs, and other NGOs; mercenary organizations, therefore, often team up with local NGOs and consulting firms to implement donor-funded projects.

BUREAUCRACY

Like all private and public organizations, aid organizations have bureaucratic problems. For donor government agencies, these problems may be compounded by their very natures. As public agencies, their efficiency is not measured by profit and must be assessed through other, less obvious management techniques. As donor agencies, their activities often consist of providing funds to support development efforts rather than directly implementing those efforts. As a result, donor agency efficiency is often assessed in terms of money spent rather than by development outcomes.[40]

The United States Agency for International Development provides an important example of the debilitating effects of bureaucracy on development assistance efforts. In its early years, USAID personnel were directly involved in implementing development activities. As a result, the organization provided opportunities for individuals who wanted to be personally involved in development. In the 1970s, USAID (like other U.S. government agencies) was subject to personnel limits, but its program was not reduced. To carry out its program without increasing its personnel levels, USAID began to implement projects through contracts with private-sector firms, and now most of its projects are implemented in this fashion. Its staff members are second-hand managers rather than first-hand implementors, and many become frustrated. They want to be directly involved in project implementation and often micro-manage project contracts, focusing on the details of internal project administration rather than on external project results. Contractor consultants, hired for their technical skills, are often overwhelmed with paperwork as a consequence.

Like all public bureaucracies, development agencies operate on budgets that are reviewed and approved, usually annually. To continue present funding levels, existing budgets must be spent, so incentives to disburse funds can supersede incentives to achieve development goals. For example, Judith Tendler argues that USAID has given high priority to U.S. export promotion in its development aid outlays because this emphasis has allowed the agency to survive in the competitive environment that exists within the federal government.[41] However, this approach conflicts with USAID's objective of promoting the private sector in developing countries. Donor agencies must live with such contradictions, which result from their multifaceted agenda to promote their own bureaucratic objectives, advance state political and economic interests, extend humanitarian development aid, and contribute to international stability.

These bureaucratic incentives on project implementation result in a focus on inputs and budgets spent rather than on sustainable outputs. Project inputs are relatively easy to control and measure, whereas outputs are often long term and difficult to quantify. Numbers of computers and vehicles are easy to count, but behavioral change—the key to long-term development—is particularly hard to measure. It is easier for forestry projects to focus on seedlings planted than on surviving trees or villagers' attitudes toward conserving and regenerating forest resources.

The focus on inputs rather than on change means donor agencies often do not know whether a particular development approach works; they only know it is efficient in spending money, and this efficiency is often mistaken for long-term success. Unfortunately, institutional learning often occurs only through the collective failures of many projects.

COORDINATING DEVELOPMENT ACTORS

How do these various development actors—states, multilateral organizations, foundations, PVOs/NGOs, and private consulting firms—reconcile their differing motivations with the need to coordinate development activities with each other? What effect do conflict and cooperation among these actors have on the recipients of development aid at the community level? Some motivations may be partially explained by some theories, but no theory adequately accounts for the multiplicity of actors and their different objectives and agenda. These objectives and agenda sometimes conflict; sometimes they are complementary. When purposes and programs converge, socioeconomic development may move forward; when they diverge, the tension may be productive if new insights result, or it may be detrimental if programs work at cross-purposes. Despite these conflicting agenda, progress often still occurs.

Many attempts have been made to understand the development process and to coordinate the programs of the principal actors. The Development Advisory Committee of the OECD sponsors studies on the overall dimensions of international development. University-based centers of development studies contribute theoretical and applied insights on the development process. The CGIAR concentrates on the technical aspects of development assistance. More analysis is needed to explain the behavior of development organizations themselves. Without such analysis, it is impossible to explain why—with all its design and delivery flaws—development aid remains a sought-after resource by host countries, why donors actively compete with each other to give money away, and why some development models are more successful than others.

Public-Sector Coordination

Since the 1950s, in recognition of the need to coordinate activities, donors—with the acquiescence of recipients—have held regular (often monthly) meetings, often convened by the UNDP and the World Bank. These meetings provide a forum for reviewing progress on economic and sector policy reforms, monitoring aid flows, and sharing information on projects to avoid duplication and conflict.

Donor meetings convened by the World Bank to coordinate the various agencies involved in the structural adjustment program in Nepal may help donors air varying political views. However, donor communication does not change the reality that Nepal will always be caught between its two powerful neighbors or that aid from other countries will likely always be influenced by political, humanitarian, and security considerations. Nepalese officials—like those from other developing countries—sometimes resist donor coordination by donors, regarding this task as their own responsibility.

Although developing countries with scarce resources cannot afford duplication in research or development projects, they often have problems coordinating internal agencies that compete rather than cooperate. In Nepal, the Ministry of Agriculture and the Institute for Agriculture and Animal Science, under the Ministry of Education, have parallel, physically adjoining commodity improvement programs that have difficulty coordinating activities. Many projects in the Philippines address forest management issues, often with overlapping terms of reference; coordinating these may not be a priority for any single project or for the government.

Competition among development organizations for influence in poor countries is commonplace; it profoundly affects these countries' development agenda and may stimulate debate in recipient governments about how much and what level of bilateral and multilateral development aid to accept. However, despite rhetoric and sincere attempts to maintain sustainable, consistent national development philosophies and purposes, rarely does a country refuse development aid simply because donors' programs conflict or overlap. As a result, donors' development project agenda often work at cross-purposes, replicate efforts, and undercut the overall effectiveness of development activities.

Private-Sector Coordination

Private organizational actors interact with both donor and recipient states in implementing development activities. The market for development is set by donor preferences through national budget allocations and the agenda of official implementing agencies, such as USAID, the Danish International Development Agency (DANIDA), the Norwegian Agency for International Development (NORAD), the Japan International Cooperation Agency (JICA), the German Agency for Technical Cooperation (GTZ), and the British Overseas Development Authority. Private organizations lobby to influence these allocations and agenda at all stages and levels of development activity, but most must eventually respond to donor budgets and agenda to obtain funding. The market for development is also influenced by recipient preferences expressed through agreements with donor states (often with local finance requirements) and private donor organizations.

PVOs/NGOs must interact with national governments, which can hinder their ability to work with the most disadvantaged, and potentially politically potent, elements of society. PVO/NGO activity in Bangladesh before 1990 focused on empowering marginal groups (the landless, women, ethnic groups), and this work was perceived as threatening the government's ability to control the population. In 1990, an NGO Affairs Bureau was created to review, control, and regulate expatriate and national PVO/NGO development work. NGOs must pay registration fees, have all projects approved by the bureau, and pay fees to implement projects. Foreign funds must be channeled through the bureau to NGO bank accounts. The bureau monitors and evaluates all projects and can terminate projects judged to be damaging national security, ignoring government regulations, or misappropriating funds.[42]

Private organizational actors also interact with each other. PVOs/NGOs and mercenary implementing organizations often cooperate to provide resources and information when implementing complementary or related projects, particularly when they face the same national government bureaucratic environment. Domestic and external competition can occur when agenda or activities conflict, such as in the quest for new contracts.

Brian Smith views PVO/NGO activities as constituting a network of private international aid that enhances the short-run political and economic stability of governments at both the sending and receiving ends.[43] In the short run, this network preserves class differentiations within the societies in which it works by postponing change through reducing pressures for more radical social restructuring. This humanitarian work harnesses the energies of middle-class citizens and can dissuade political dissidents from taking more radical action.

This network may help maintain the system of international development, partly because it is an outlet for potentially subversive political energies in both donor and recipient countries. It uses these energies to serve the immediate interests of political and economic elites in both donor and recipient states.

Although multiple agenda are pursued simultaneously by donors and implementing agencies, these various objectives result in a creative tension that gives international development assistance organizations an incentive to continually evaluate current models of implementation and to search for new models. International development organizations are able to function because overlapping (in addition to competing) goals are held by public and private organizations that provide a common ground for consensus.

CONCLUSION

Power and the intensely political reactions its quest evokes can never be divorced from development aid, which is used by donor and recipient states to influence each other, enhance international stability, and improve the quality of people's lives. The challenge for development practitioners is to channel this aid into projects that alleviate poverty through sustainable agricultural, industrial, or service-sector activities.

Power politics among states can affect village life for all economic classes through markets for imported goods, availability of agricultural inputs (seeds, fertilizer, irrigation equipment), provision of electricity, delivery of health care, and funding for schools. Domestic politics influence the areas that will receive development funds and the groups that will benefit from training. Additionally, donors often prefer to focus their efforts on the one sector (agriculture, education, health, infrastructure, or credit) in which they believe these efforts will be most effective.

Abuse of the political nature of development can lead to misguided projects that hurt targeted recipients. Development programs designed by donors have missed the importance of subsistence agriculture and have placed too much emphasis on mechanizing agriculture; they have also ignored input delivery, the role of women, the need to develop markets, and the significance of informal welfare networks among rural people.

Nevertheless, humanitarian motivations to extend development aid are usually present even in obviously political situations. Development projects are designed and implemented by people who genuinely want to help others improve their lives. Disaster relief, which has a shorter time horizon than development aid, is also influenced by politics, although NGOs and PVOs often try to develop infrastructure that can be sustained by local organizations.

The political dilemma of development aid is concerned with the motivations of states and organizations and with the interactions between them. Regardless of their size, states and organizations are made up of people, and the processes and outcomes of development aid—whether political or humanitarian, provided for selfish or altruistic objectives—are influenced by the people who implement aid-funded activities. In Chapter 4 we address the personal dimension of development aid by examining the dilemma of choosing between expatriate and national professionals to implement development activities.

FOUR

□ □ □

The Individual Dilemma:
Who Should Implement
Development?

I returned to Nepal ten years after the end of my Peace Corps assignment, this time as the research specialist for a program called Strengthening Institutional Capacity in the Food and Agricultural Sector. The objective of this program was to improve policy decisions in agricultural and rural development through enhancing social science research, economic analysis, and information management capacity in His Majesty's government and other concerned organizations. This was to be achieved by increasing the number of competent individual analysts, administrators, and researchers. Funding for the program was provided by USAID, the Ford Foundation, the German Agency for Technical Cooperation (GTZ), and the Canadian International Development Research Centre (IDRC) to be used for graduate degree training, nondegree training, research projects, seminars, and workshops.

The program's implementing agency was the Agricultural Development Council, a private organization funded largely by the Rockefeller family, which later merged into the Winrock International Institute for Agricultural Development—the largest PVO working in agricultural development. The counterpart agency in Nepal was the Agricultural Projects Services Center, which was created to expand local capacity to conduct agricultural project analysis and provide other technical services for Nepal's development efforts. I worked with another expatriate, the program leader, to implement the program.

The program had a budget of about $500,000 per year—modest by development aid standards. To increase individual and institutional capability, this budget provided funding for graduate degrees in social science fields related to agricultural and natural resource management. Fellowship recipients were expected to address policy-related issues in their graduate research. Nondegree, short-term training in Nepal and nearby countries was intended to increase skills in basic management, computer operation, environmental studies, project analysis, and rural development management.

Some funding was provided for in-country research. Most was used for small studies (with budgets under $1,000, lasting less than a year) conducted by individual researchers.

89

Although the quality of the research varied, over 80 research studies were completed on a wide variety of agricultural and natural resource management topics. The results of many of these efforts were published by the project and distributed to interested professionals in Nepal and around the world.

Both the training and research activities of this project were labor-intensive: It takes time to solicit, screen, and select candidates for degree fellowships and even more time to review research proposals, monitor research progress, and edit research papers for publication. The underlying philosophy of the project was that these investments would pay handsome dividends in the long run: By training and encouraging individuals, Nepal's public and private institutions concerned with managing the country's agricultural and natural resources would be better equipped to solve the problems resulting from increasing demands on these resources.

This was a long-term philosophy: The people selected for graduate degree training today may not make significant contributions to problem solving for many years after they return to Nepal. Some may decide private-sector consulting is more rewarding intellectually and financially than government service, and some may have opportunities to work for international organizations after they finish their graduate training. However, the skills of such individuals are not lost to society—they may be temporarily unavailable to Nepal's public sector, but they continue to serve world development. A broad perspective, and a long-term vision, are needed to sustain efforts in human resource development.

A long-term vision was also needed to cope with the pace of government activity. Procedures that should have taken a few days often stretched into months without action. The practice of passing files from lower-level offices up through agency hierarchies for official decisionmaking ensured that nearly everyone concerned was consulted; it also provided the opportunity for delay by junior officials and the possibility for corruption at many stages in the process. The strong family orientation of Nepalese society resulted in personal pressures in many aspects of official activity.

In Nepal, the university system has been weak, despite the dedication of some faculty members. Aspiring professionals aim for foreign degrees because they have more prestige both nationally and internationally. Unfortunately, the cost of these degrees is within the reach of few Nepalis; the only alternative is to compete for the limited number of scholarships given by foreign donors.

Each year when the graduate fellowships were announced, there was intense competition for the limited number of awards. Although applications were welcome from both public officials and private individuals, government restrictions (from both the United States and Nepal) limited eligibility for the USAID-funded fellowships to officials from certain government agencies and, further, to those who received permission to apply. Preliminary screening and interviews took place in Kathmandu, and final selection was made by an international committee that met in Bangkok to make similar selections for fellowship programs in several Asian countries. The final selection was done offshore to avoid potential local political pressure.

Even with the final selection being made in Bangkok, local pressure was exerted to recommend candidates from a variety of government agencies associated with the Ministry of Agriculture, although the quality of the candidates from some agencies was usually weak. Should weaker candidates be selected in order to improve the capacity of these agencies, or should individual merit be the sole criterion for selection?

My goal was to work myself out of a job and to have a Nepali be the research specialist. I believed expatriates—particularly individuals assigned for only a few years at a time—could never completely understand the intricacies and needs of Nepal's society and that it was thus in Nepal's long-term self-interest to be completely in charge of its own development. The program leader and I made a conscious effort to involve Nepalese professionals in all stages of the research grant and fellowship award process, and they played an increasing role in project implementation. Panels of Nepalese professionals were created to assist with the selection processes for both fellowships and research awards. In their own jobs, these professionals may have made less than one-tenth of my salary.

I left Nepal after nearly six years, with the program having successfully met or exceeded the training and research objectives set for the period 1982–1987. Funding for another five-year phase of the program was assured from USAID and the Ford Foundation. The research specialist position had been designated for a Nepalese professional, with a new expatriate as the program leader.

As was the case in the village, development in government agencies occurs along many dimensions. I attempted to help improve the quality of research related to agricultural production and natural resource management. While working with government agencies for more than five years, I also tried to provide an example of different office procedures, with different values; some would call them efficient, others might call them impersonal. The government officials likewise provided an example to me. As in the village, exposure to official procedures and perspectives is important for expatriates working in development if they are to find acceptable solutions to government problems.

When I left Kathmandu, I again illustrated that expatriates can go home and escape the problems of development. Whatever my dedication, I never had the same stake in the success or failure of development activities as the Nepalis do. Nevertheless, donors continue to prefer placing expatriates in some key program and project positions, particularly those concerned with finances. Can expatriates work themselves out of jobs when those jobs are funded with donor money? What do expatriates offer that nationals do not (and vice versa)?

How does socioeconomic development occur? Although economic and political theories have some explanatory power, they simplify in order to explain. As described in Chapter 2, economic development theory often discusses economic aggregates (such as income, food production, and employment) and ignores the individual organizations and people associated with those aggregates. Socioeconomic development occurs when sufficient capital is accumulated for long-term investment (the aggregate view); it also occurs when individuals are motivated to save and to make investments in their own countries (the personal view). In many developing country situations, these investments may simply use human and physical resources on a more sustainable basis, thereby preventing the further degradation of these resources.

Similarly, as discussed in Chapter 3, international relations theory tends to focus on political aggregates (such as states), ignoring the individual organizations and people that comprise those aggregates. Socioeconomic development occurs when it serves states' interests; it also occurs when individuals take political action to improve their personal welfare. Discussions of international development often focus on states, because they usually control most development resources. However, states do not control all development resources; in particular, they cannot completely control information, the most important such resource. Empowered with information that helps them understand the use of resources and technology, people will change their lives with or without states.

THE PERSONALITY OF DEVELOPMENT

Like states and private organizations, individuals exert influence at their own levels. Because both states and organizations are represented by and act only through individuals, individuals exert influence on all levels of foreign aid and development activities.

Bureaucratic conflicts over control of development complicate implementation decisions, which might otherwise be resolved in favor of administrative efficiency. With limited human resources, individual personalities can be important factors. Whom do donors want to implement development projects? Whom do recipients want? Who can best ensure technical success and long-term sustainability? Who can best ensure the transfer of technology and skills to target beneficiaries? These questions must be asked continually to help focus project objectives. If a project trains foresters in agroforestry techniques so they can transfer these skills to male and female farmers, is it more appropriate to work with national consultants who are well acquainted with the country's specific—and perhaps unique—agroecological systems or with expatriate consultants who have experience transferring this technology in several countries?

This is the individual dilemma of socioeconomic development—to choose between expatriates and national individuals in allocating control of the development process and to determine who has the power to make that choice. In this chapter we analyze the roles of individuals in implementing development activities. We focus on the question, Who can best implement development?

Individuals exert influence on all levels of foreign aid and development activities; here, Nepalese farmers with sacks of fertilizer. (Photo by Richard Hawkins, courtesy of Winrock International)

More specifically, are expatriates or nationals better suited to implement development activities? How can these individuals work together to implement projects and achieve development goals? Is it more efficient to help the elite to help the poor, or is it better to work directly with the poor, even if only a fraction can be reached with limited resources? Are gender issues important to consider in staffing and in project design, implementation, and evaluation?

Development project budgets are carefully reviewed by donors and recipient governments. Expatriate salaries are high, national professional salaries are rising, and resources to achieve development goals are limited. Choices between expatriate and national individuals have significant implications for the size of project budgets and control of the development process.

The selection of project implementors involves control and ownership of the development process and products. Should expatriate technical assistance be used to implement projects quickly, or is the slower pace of local participation more effective in the long run? How should practitioners choose among expatriate technical competence, national expertise, and local empowerment? How should they decide between the traditional male-female roles and newer variations that may be more effective in project implementation? These complicating political factors transform administrative problems into practical implementation dilemmas.

In this chapter we discuss the dilemma of human resource development, the key to stimulating socioeconomic development. We describe the motivations of expatriate advisers, national professionals, and local villagers involved in development projects. Individual objectives and motivations interact with each other and with the agenda of states and multilateral organizations and complicate implementation of development projects.

Development professionals must decide on the appropriate combination of individuals and organizations—expatriates and nationals, men and women—to implement development projects. These actors are the key to effectively reaching the poor people who are the intended beneficiaries of development.

Countries often go through several stages of development and development aid; these are interactive steps involving both donor perceptions and recipient needs. First, aid is provided to build physical infrastructure (roads, buildings, laboratories); second, funds are needed to increase individual human abilities (technical skills and degree training); third, budgets are sought for institutions and systems (management skills and nondegree training); and fourth, money alone is provided (with responsibility and authority in the hands of recipients).

Similarly, relations between expatriate and national organizations often go through several stages. First, projects are implemented through expatriate firms; second, expatriate firms engage national firms as junior partners; third, national firms take the lead, with expatriate firms as junior partners; and fourth, national firms take the entire responsibility for implementing projects.

What are appropriate and effective roles (and relationships with host country colleagues) for expatriate advisers as developing countries advance? An examination of the history of human resource development in poor countries provides some insights into possible answers.

HUMAN RESOURCE DEVELOPMENT

Millions of dollars have been spent to train individuals from developing countries and to improve technical training institutions in these countries. The Rockefeller Foundation and the Ford Foundation have played primary roles in shaping human resource development programs around the world, particularly since World War II. Many bilateral and multilateral donors sponsor degree training programs; some reserve special funds for fellowships, such as the Japan Special Fund at the Asian Development Bank.

Prior to World War II, academic and technical training for people in developing countries was supported through colonial relationships or private philanthropic efforts. The Rockefeller Foundation, founded in the early twentieth century with revenues from the Standard Oil Corporation, was for many years the most influential and effective of such organizations. This foundation invested substantial resources in scientific research and education with the firm belief that these resources could "promote the well-being of humankind throughout the world."[1] Concentrating on promoting medical research on tropical diseases and training Chinese doctors, the Rockefeller foundation developed training models and a philosophy of human resource development. These ideas and models were echoed in Rockefeller efforts in Latin America, Thailand, and the rest of Asia, as well as by the Ford Foundation and official U.S. aid after World War II.[2]

The United States emerged from World War II as the world's richest and strongest country, in part because Britain and other European powers were unable to control their overseas colonial possessions. Independence movements gained strength in these colonies, and with Indian independence and the Chinese Communist revolution, new socioeconomic development models became possible. Following implementation of the Marshall Plan, in which American economists and technical experts played key roles in using investment as a primary tool for reconstruction, the United States was in a unique position to influence the path taken by developing countries. The Marshall Plan spent $12 billion in 19 countries with varied results, but overall it was a success in rebuilding and rejuvenating war-damaged European economies.

Having just emerged from its own Great Depression, the United States viewed poverty as a malady that could be overcome with the proper infusion of knowledge and capital. Poverty was seen as resulting from the lack of technically trained individuals who were able to address sectoral growth problems and from the lack of capital to finance investments. U.S. idealism about its ability to help poor countries alleviate poverty stemmed from its roles in the creation of the League of Nations and the United Nations, as well as from its long relationships with China, East Asia, and Latin America, which combined both trade and economic interests with idealistic missionary and philanthropic objectives.[3]

As combatting the spread of communism became more political, newly independent countries became the testing ground for U.S. and European theories of economic growth and development. The Soviet Union and the new People's Republic of China responded in kind (although Chinese development aid did not begin until some years after the revolution) with fellowship programs, technical assistance, and infrastructural programs of their own. These programs were presented as alternatives to the programs funded by capitalist countries, which had been colonial powers in many poor countries. For example, India has received assistance from both the former Soviet Union and the United Kingdom.

The Rockefeller Foundation and the Ford Foundation, along with the U.S. government, began intensive development efforts in Asia. Asia was an active area for development efforts during the period 1950–1970, with the Soviet Union, China, and the United States competing for influence in South and Southeast Asia. The transfer of knowledge was seen as key to the development puzzle in Asia—foreign experts were mobilized to help advise governments, national educational institutions were created or strengthened, and thousands of nationals were sent to developed countries for short-term and long-term training in agriculture, biology, engineering, economics, and rural social sciences.

The model developed through the Rockefeller Foundation's experience was based on the premise that with "proper" training—in the United States and later in Western Europe, Japan, Australia, and some institutions in Thailand, the Philippines, and Malaysia—individuals would return to their own countries and contribute to the development process. These individuals—with the benefit of their training and experience in more "advanced" socioeconomic environments—would assume leadership positions, make policies, conduct research, and teach in ways that would stimulate economic growth, foster democracy, and alleviate poverty.[4]

It was assumed that having experienced and learned a "better" way, these men and women would share their knowledge easily with other ethnic groups and would be willing to work directly with poor people. Nongovernmental organizations, such as the Rockefeller-funded Agricultural Development Council, were dedicated to identifying potential leaders for advanced degree training, strengthening local educational institutions, stimulating research on important development topics, and helping scholars who had returned to their home environments readjust after completing their studies.

Although many dedicated and skilled individuals were trained, donors were slow to recognize the limitations of this human resource development model:

□ Local professionals have personal motivations.
□ Institutional strengthening is complicated by politics.
□ Social change takes time.
□ Each country has its own unique economic and social relationships.

Individuals such as this Nepalese professional at work on a human resources development project—with the benefit of training and experience in more "advanced" socioeconomic environments—do not always assume leadership positions in their own countries. (Photo by Melissa Yazman, courtesy of Winrock International)

First, those who could easily meet the qualifications for training in Western schools were the wealthy elite, who had the requisite secondary school training and language skills. These individuals, although perhaps truly concerned for their countries' development and the plight of poor people, had little incentive to extend their knowledge and wealth to less advantaged groups. Many who returned with dreams of participating in significant socioeconomic change or technological discoveries were frustrated by archaic bureaucracies, low pay, lack of funding for research, professional jealousies, and societies that did not appreciate their overseas experiences.

This model also assumed that members of this group wanted to emulate the West. Although many gained respect for Western cultures and appreciated their educations, few jettisoned their own cultural heritage for Western ways. Many returned home and pursued national economic development without jeopardizing their own socioeconomic positions. Returnees who were frustrated by local institutional and social constraints often opted for more lucrative and professionally rewarding positions in international organizations.

Second, institutional strengthening—a key component in this model—is not a straightforward process. Donors recognized that individuals alone were unlikely to change moribund national agencies, but institution-strengthening efforts were given insufficient resources to transform entire national research and training systems. Selected agricultural ministries might receive research funds, new buildings, and expatriate technical assistance, only to suffer politically from the jealousies of other ministries. Few governments could match donor inputs for strengthening institutions, so expectations of improving many ministries or universities were unfulfilled. Foreign fellowships are expensive, and countries need their own strong, degree-granting institutions in order to develop. Without people willing to work for low salaries and to overcome political jealousies, these institutions have remained weak.

Recognizing the difficulty of transforming entire national research, extension, and teaching systems, in the early 1960s donors created international agricultural research centers to conduct desperately needed research to improve agricultural production in tropical areas and to serve as homes for scientists who had left their countries out of frustration. These centers have been profoundly successful in improving agricultural production, but, ironically, this very success may have weakened national institutions; top national scientists have been recruited to work at the international centers, and donor financial resources have supported the international centers rather than national institutions.

Third, although economic growth can occur quickly (Southeast Asia is a good example), social change takes more time—perhaps generations. Developing country governments and donors have been slow to understand the pace of this change. Communist governments in Eastern Europe and the former Soviet Union have learned this lesson the hard way, and the Chinese government continues to struggle with this realization.

Fourth, the pristine conditions for development often assumed by donor and recipient governments never existed. Each developing country has its own unique history (as do developed countries), with complex economic and social relationships among various classes of people and ethnic groups, different histories of economic production, different natural resource endowments, and different contacts with other countries. Socioeconomic development in poor, agricultural countries is more complicated than is rebuilding war-torn European industrial economies.

Critical decisions must be made by governments and people about which development model to follow, which resources to develop, standards of political and economic rights, domestic distributive justice, investment policies, international trade, and relations with development donors. None of these decisions is easy for any society, and the post–World War II environment presented particularly complex issues involving newly independent states, international debt, natural resource extraction, common property access, pollution, and militarization that demanded unprecedented national action and international cooperation. Initially, this complexity was not appreciated by donors, which accounts for the dilemmas faced by recipient governments and donors regarding the "ownership" of development projects.

The individual dilemma of development assistance arises because, despite the rhetoric and the millions of dollars spent on training, donors are still more comfortable with their own analysis and interpretation of development problems and with expatriates' capacity to foster economic change and resist corruption than they are with local analysis and implementation. Human resource development efforts were expected to increase national capacity to address development issues; however, for the reasons discussed above, these efforts have not resulted in the quick returns envisioned by donors. Nevertheless, despite its flaws, this human resource model is the primary way by which donors and developing countries have increased the number of skilled individuals and strengthened national research and training institutions. This model, oriented toward training advantaged individuals in the belief that they are the best equipped to initiate fundamental socioeconomic change, is optimistic.

Although members of the elite classes trained through this model have made substantial contributions to the national and international understanding of agriculture, economics, and development, relying on a trickle-down model for information and technology transfer to combat worsening rural poverty is quixotic. The need for knowledge and technology transfer is acute, but the wisdom and experience of small landholders (the predominant farming population in poor countries) must also be appreciated by scientists and national planners and be incorporated into scientific research and national agenda for this knowledge and technology to be successfully applied in rural areas.

Critical of the elite model, since the 1960s international and national PVOs/NGOs have experimented with bottom-up models of training and technology transfer that are faithful to local conditions and driven by locally articulated needs. This alternative view of human resource development places leadership for development in the hands of those providing food and using natural resources. It relies on the transformation of traditional structures by local people, using their own knowledge as the basis for change.

Donors and implementing organizations have gradually realized that participatory cooperation is the best mode for achieving development, both for institutions and for individuals. Unfortunately, this discovery has not yet significantly affected relations between donor and recipient states, in which recipient countries still have few opportunities to work in partnership with bilateral or multilateral donors in developing and evaluating projects.

Experience with socioeconomic development since World War II shows it is a complex process that, following the Western model, is almost impossible for countries to undertake on their own. Exchanges of ideas, technology, and capital are needed to create institutions, improve agricultural production and natural resource management, build infrastructure and industry, and reform policy. National and expatriate roles are constantly evolving. An examination of personal motives in development assistance indicates that addressing the individual dilemma may now be the key to development.

INDIVIDUAL MOTIVES

Individuals are important in donor and recipient state agencies, private implementing organizations, and villages. Individuals working in donor agencies design projects and request proposals from private-sector organizations and PVOs/NGOs; individuals working in implementing organizations respond with their own ideas and often initiate proposals themselves; implementation is carried out by individuals; and the purpose of development efforts is to improve the lives of individuals.

Who can best implement development activities—expatriates or national professionals? Some nationals worry that development projects implemented by expatriates will have neocolonial or neoimperial overtones, with foreigners telling nationals how to run their own countries. There is concern that using expatriates deprives nationals of jobs and the opportunity to gain valuable experience. Other nationals want expatriates because these outsiders can often act without being constrained by local cultural norms and social obligations. The belief persists that such ties are stronger in poor countries than in rich, but these ties may have simply been replaced by other loyalties. In addition, many people—expatriates and nationals, donors and recipients—believe it is difficult to control corruption without the supervision of expatriates.

Among nationals, who can best design and implement development activities—professionals or beneficiaries? Professional skills may be needed to solve technical problems, but familiarity with local social constraints may be as important in designing effective solutions to these problems. Just as most expatriates do not have the same long-term personal stake in development as do national professionals, and the national professionals have less of a stake than the beneficiaries.

What motivates individuals to participate in development? As indicated above, three categories of people are important in development efforts: expatriates, national professionals, and beneficiaries. These categories are discussed in the next three sections.

Expatriates

What motivates expatriates to participate in development? What is the effect of including them in project implementation? Expatriates serve as short-term or long-term advisers, with terms ranging from a few weeks to several years; they have important roles in policymaking and in project funding, design, and implementation. As with any career, the personal and professional objectives of expatriate advisers are intertwined. These motivations include:

□ Humanitarian, altruistic, and ideological concerns for poor people
□ Desire for money and power
□ Desire for social status and high living standards
□ Opportunity for travel and diverse cultural experiences
□ Professional and personal development goals
□ Escape from confining careers or life-styles at home

Senior expatriate development professionals have often worked in several regions of the world and can share lessons learned from various agroecosystems, cultures, and levels of development. However, there is a limit to generalizations across countries and cultures, and few professionals believe all poor countries are similar. Expatriates often move among donor agencies, PVOs/NGOs, and consulting firms, and a seasoned professional who has worked for only one organization is rare.

The diverse experience of expatriates gives them the capacity to be flexible, to understand and articulate broad visions, and to share technologies and ideas across cultures and national borders. Unfortunately, experience with many failures can also make expatriates cynical and less willing to be sensitive to local traditions and power relationships.

The ability of development professionals to interact with host country nationals is critical to successful implementation. People with backgrounds in voluntary service organizations, such as the U.S. Peace Corps (Canada, Japan, the Netherlands, and the United Kingdom also have volunteer organizations, as does the United Nations), have an advantage in this regard. They have village-level experience, know local languages, and have compassion for disadvantaged and poor people. They have firsthand knowledge of the effectiveness of local branches of national bureaucracies and of PVOs/NGOs.

Experience has shown that effective expatriate roles are those based on cooperative co-learning, working together to solve problems that have been identified by national officials and donor agencies. International development is fraught with examples of projects that failed because partnerships were not formed between expatriate professionals and national bureaucrats. Even if institutions (such as expatriate consulting firms paying low wages to national project staff) are reluctant to support such partnerships, success is possible if the interaction is participatory.

Project leaders are often key to project success and to good relationships between expatriates and national staff members. These leaders influence project implementation and can affect success through their ability to get along with national counterparts while at the same time addressing the concerns of national bureaucracies, the requirements of donors, and the goals of their own institutions (consulting firms, universities, PVOs/NGOs). The ability to work in difficult and impoverished environments, be culturally sensitive, and remain optimistic is critical to project success.

Project leaders are also key to ensuring that gender-related project goals are emphasized. Most leaders are men from rich countries; this is slowly changing to include expatriate men from poorer countries, national male professionals, and expatriate women from rich countries. Few women from poor countries are project leaders, either in their own countries or as expatriates.

However personally or professionally committed or cooperative expatriates may be, they have no stake in the process or the outcome of projects and do not have to live with the results of their work. However, expatriates are also not caught in local social or political webs that constrain thinking and action in many development projects. In particular, expatriates are believed to have less political objectives than those of national experts, and thus they will not likely become mired in bureaucratic corruption, payoffs, and embezzlement. Development projects sometimes inject massive amounts of foreign currency and goods into an economy. This infusion is attractive to national governments, which usually receive some of the funds. Project budgets are often controlled by expatriates in the belief that this will avoid misuse of funds. Donors generally view expatriates as being less corruptible because they are paid international salaries and need not worry about money, which is one reason they are often preferred as project leaders.

Misuse of funds, bribery, and even embezzlement are difficult to control in development projects. Although corruption is often viewed as an artifact of weak government, it exists in both strong and weak governments that lack well-established procedures for accountability.[5] Corruption occurs because national government budgets are small and overextended. Government personnel are poorly paid and frequently moonlight in consulting or other businesses to increase their incomes. Development projects have money, and the temptation to skim off the top, or to require extra payments for routine procedures, can be irresistible for national officials.

Corruption is difficult to control and track in environments that lack procedural reliability and accountability of public servants at every level. Coralie Bryant and Louise White argue that political corruption is an intrinsic part of development and social change rather than an indication of cultural malady. When rapid social and economic changes occur, the boundaries between social norms and legal rules become blurred. England in the sixteenth century and the United States in the nineteenth century experienced high levels of corruption during periods of rapid socioeconomic change. Bryant and White claim that enhancing the self-esteem of lower-level officials, and developing support mechanisms to reward them for good performance, will reduce corruption and increase their responsiveness to clients' needs.[6] However, as long as development donors continue to provide resources that far exceed those of their local counterparts (which, after all, is the purpose of much development), the temptation and possibility for corruption will remain.

Individuals are subject to personal and social constraints resulting from institutional pressures on their careers, which may lead to behavioral deviations. Many development officials rationalize repression or corruption that would be impossible to overlook in their own societies or personal philosophies. For example, a U.S. citizen who feels strongly about human rights may find a development job with a repressive government and rationalize this by believing the work is doing some good.

In general, expatriate development workers and professionals tend to be immune from some of the social and political forces constraining national policymakers, and they can, and sometimes do, make statements government officials cannot. We can only hope that national decisionmakers in developing countries have the good sense to embrace the enlightened and reject the ridiculous from among expatriate exhortations.

Anticipating and articulating host country needs are continual problems for both donor agency staff and recipient country officials. As development proceeds, the number of technically trained host country professionals increases, and the need for outside technical assistance diminishes. Individual training and institutional-strengthening programs are designed to increase the skills of government officials so national professionals can perform development tasks previously carried out by expatriates; their implicit objective is to have national organizations and individuals eventually put expatriates out of business. However, expatriate individuals and organizations survive by engaging in international development consulting, and they are reluctant to relinquish this lucrative source of income. Donors must address the conflict inherent in the dual objective of helping poor recipient countries and providing opportunities for their own domestic businesses.

With the growing technical expertise of nationals, the need for expatriate advisers has been questioned. Why do donor agencies and national bureaucracies still want expatriates to implement development projects? Expanding policy agenda in developing countries are sometimes influenced by expatriate advisers whose worldview is less fatalistic than are the culturally accepted norms in these countries; until rigid hierarchies and fatalistic viewpoints become less common, expatriates may continue to be helpful in redefining organizational and individual perspectives and agenda. However, the roles of expatriates themselves must also be continually redefined to respond to the changing needs of recipient countries.

National Professionals

What are the primary motivations that cause national individuals to participate in development projects? National professionals often help expatriates with policymaking and with project design and implementation. In fact, the list of motivations for national actors is the same as that given on p. 101 for expatriates, but the context is different. National professionals may have few other opportunities for high salaries or even for employment that uses their technical skills, for professional training and development, for contact with expatriate experts in their professional fields, for regular access to advanced technology (computers, scientific equipment, and even vehicles), or to help achieve needed change.

Unfortunately—as in developed countries—individual incentives do not always match national needs. Midway through the Nepalese project described at the beginning of this chapter, individuals who had completed degrees (mostly M.A.s) under earlier phases of the project were surveyed to assess the long-term effects of these training programs and to help improve future training efforts. The most common answers to two questions were revealing:

> **Q:** What skills learned in your M.A. degree training do you use on a regular basis?
> **A:** None. I am too busy with administrative work.
> **Q:** What can this program do to best help you in your career?
> **A:** Provide Ph.D. training.

These answers give some insight into the problems that pervade development implementation. Administration of project details overwhelms thinking about program purpose and effect, and short-term deadlines overwhelm long-term goals. Individual motivations for personal career advancement take precedence over national needs. One key to achieving long-term development objectives is to align individual incentives with organizational and national goals. In economic terms, the individual and social costs and benefits of development activities must coincide in order to eliminate unwanted results.

The benefits of working on donor-funded development projects often encourage internal brain drains, as talented professionals are lured to work for high-paying donors rather than for recipient governments. Despite this tendency, their professional allegiance usually remains with national priorities rather than being transferred to those of donors or expatriate implementing agencies. The benefits of expatriates and nationals working together include the exchange of ideas and exposure to different management styles. Recipient governments also benefit by having national staff implementing projects rather than professionally stagnating in ministries that have few resources and weak political support. However, external brain drains often result from salaries being higher in industrial countries and international organizations than in poor countries. Well-paying in-country consulting opportunities make it easier for highly trained individuals to stay in their own countries to work.

Many middle-income developing countries—such as Indonesia, Mexico, Nigeria, and the Philippines—already have skilled technicians and scientists to staff national institutions and do not need technical assistance from foreign experts. Universities in these countries attract students from other developing countries, and donors fund students to study at these schools. Yet these countries, for all their trained individuals and capacity for human resource development, are often unable to mobilize private-sector capital to finance development efforts. They have the capital to develop but have been unable to convince their elites to invest these resources in national development efforts.

Many national professionals, whose personal objectives differ from official state goals, work with NGOs out of frustration with the slowness of government to address equity issues and the causes of poverty. This middle-class group has played an important role in working with both rural and urban poor people. For example, Sally W. Yudelman documents five Central American grass-roots–oriented development groups that owe their origins to socially progressive Catholics and middle-class and upper-class professionals.[7]

The positive role nationals can play is illustrated by the Philippine Upland Development Program, funded by the Ford Foundation and implemented by Winrock International. The program, begun in the early 1980s, focuses on developing participatory approaches to managing upland (mountain) forests and increasing the capacity of the Department of Environment and Natural Resources (DENR) to manage these uplands. Ethnic and tribal groups are using slash-and-burn (swidden) agriculture to farm upland forests, which are under DENR's jurisdiction. The challenge is to conserve the forests by developing and following forest management plans while providing more secure tenure and livelihoods for upland residents.

A key element of the program is the DENR-based Upland Development Working Group, composed of DENR officials and academic and NGO researchers and professionals. Although these groups of experts have varying opinions about upland development, the working group provides program direction and uses information and lessons to help design policies, tactical briefs, and manuals for participatory upland development. An Upland NGO Assistance Committee is responsible for promoting agroforestry and improving local people's land tenure.

The program adviser—a Filipino—by virtue of external funding (the Ford Foundation through Winrock International, a PVO), has great license to work with the various agenda represented within the working group. He is skilled in working with uplands people and has international stature as an expert on social forestry and upland development. The adviser's personal qualities, his experience with each organization in the working group, and his commitment to participatory methods have contributed to program success. In this case, the individual attributes of a national professional contribute directly to program success and sustainability. Donors are recognizing that there are many such people in developing countries.

It is often difficult for highly trained nationals to earn internationally competitive salaries as consultants. Even when nationals from developing countries have worked in other countries, they may encounter resistance at home. Donors and expatriate consulting firms are often reluctant to pay nationals at international rates because they have "returned home." This bias creates the impression that development consulting has its own caste system. A slow trickle of national project leaders for donor-funded projects is helping to change this perception.

Beneficiaries

Why do villagers cooperate with development projects when they are often justifiably suspicious of outsiders and wary of government corruption? Why do they let outsiders meddle with fragile life-styles based on dwindling resource bases?

Recipient poor people (both villagers and urban dwellers), the intended beneficiaries of many development efforts, are likely to have objectives that differ from either the political concerns of the state or the professional goals of the middle class. These objectives are primarily to increase food production and improve their standard of living.

Some villagers want and welcome government-funded development projects, some avoid them, and most have no choice in whether to accept them. If approached properly, with projects to empower people rather than trying to change them, the mix of money, technical assistance, and tradition (the experience of lifetimes) can be a happy combination.

Most donor and recipient governments consider development to be a state activity, rarely viewing what people do on their own as "development." People, whether urban or rural, are motivated to participate in socioeconomic change when they realize their current practices are not satisfying even their bare minimum basic needs. Individual initiative is the key to the development process. Development observers and practitioners have long puzzled over the best approach to encourage people to participate in official development efforts.

In Eastern Europe and the former Soviet Union, socialist systems failed as a result of economic stagnation and crisis. Despite the history of repression in these states, people forced political change from a system that was weaker than was generally realized. Although the distribution of power and reorganization of these economies is ongoing, change occurred primarily because people wanted to improve their welfare beyond what states could do for them.

The village of Ben Suc in Viet Nam is another example of local initiative. Most Western donors stopped giving aid to Viet Nam following the U.S. defeat in 1973 and Viet Nam's later invasion of Cambodia. Although some Western governments and NGOs continued to provide aid to Viet Nam's government, the main supplier of aid was the USSR. Most aid was used to rebuild major infrastructure rather than for village-level development. In 1967, Ben Suc was destroyed by U.S. forces; by 1992 people had reestablished a small village of subsistence rice farmers and rubber plantation workers.

The village had been a major staging ground for the Viet Cong, who lived among the people and won their confidence. After the U.S. attack, surviving villagers were resettled in nearby villages and given rice, but no land, by government forces. Ordered by the new government to return to their former homes, refugees from villages like Ben Suc slowly began to return, finding a wasteland. The Ben Suc villagers rebuilt their homes, replanted the fields and trees, and live much the way they did before—farming rice, harvesting cashews, and working on rubber plantations. A significant feature of the village, which may have contributed to its revival, is the fact that villagers were allowed to farm plots individually rather than collectively.

Although Ben Suc is poor, its people had the initiative to rebuild their former lives with little help from any outside agency, including the new government. Perhaps the most significant lesson to be gleaned from this

Poor people often have effective local organizations, such as this Pakistani farmers' group, for specific functions. (Photo by Michael Dove, courtesy of Winrock International)

example is that despite war and revolution, the village itself remained the most relevant model for socioeconomic development by its former inhabitants.[8]

Stereotypical rural villagers are seen as resistant to change, conservative, and suspicious of outsiders—including people from different regions of their own countries. Participatory development implementation models and research methods have shown how wrong this view of rural people can be. Many villagers are conservative as a result of living at subsistence levels, not because of an inherent lack of initiative or curiosity. To the extent that expatriates have been successful in working with rural and urban poor people, success has occurred through participatory perspectives and the willingness to learn from others, including villagers. National bureaucrats have bad reputations—some richly deserved—because social structures sometimes make it easy for them to act superior toward uneducated, but highly skilled, villagers.

Poor people often have effective local organizations for specific functions. What they may lack are the additional resources, information, and technology to cope with rapidly changing environments or increasing population pressure on fragile resources.[9] People in these local organizations are motivated to work on donor-funded development projects when

Gender analysis has been developed to ensure the inclusion of women in the design, implementation, and evaluation of development projects. Here, male and female scientists interview a female farmer as part of gender analysis data collection. (Courtesy of International Rice Research Institute)

they see clear short-term and long-term benefits and when the extra work required for projects does not disrupt their daily subsistence activities.

Despite the best intentions of expatriate and national development professionals, the impetus for official development rarely comes from poor people; they are too busy merely surviving. To address this situation, participatory methods have been developed for agriculture, fisheries, natural resources, and health. These approaches rely on the collaboration of project implementors and beneficiaries to define problems, assess available resources, and design interventions.[10] Farming systems research and extension and agroecosystem analysis combine the expertise of farmers and scientists to assess biophysical and socioeconomic constraints to interventions. Gender analysis has been developed to ensure the inclusion of women in the design, implementation, and evaluation of development projects.

Development occurs when people act to improve their own welfare. The energy and will invested by individuals in political change in Eastern Europe and in reconstruction in Ben Suc are key to economic development. This energy and will are not easily harnessed; the perceived payoff must be great. People must find time away from the daily battle of subsistence living to think about their resources and how they use them. Once men and women begin to think about what they are doing, they must talk with each other using a common frame of reference. It is here that development aid organizations and individuals—nationals and expatriates, men and women—can play effective roles.

GENDER ISSUES

How do individuals interact with each other? In development work, expatriate-expatriate, expatriate-national, and national-national relationships are all sensitive. The effect of cross-cultural relationships between expatriate advisers and national professional and support staff can be profound. This interaction can be exciting, but it can also have unintended negative effects. One source of worry for expatriates and nationals is that gender issues arise when men and women work together. Men's and women's motivations and perspectives for working in international development may be different, because women tend to focus on equity more than men do.[11]

Expatriate women are often treated as a breed apart on development projects. Rarely do development projects employ expatriate women as long-term consultants; short-term work is more common, and—even with advanced training—expatriate women rarely have power or control over project budgets. National male professionals who have few female professional peers either treat expatriate women as if they were national women (and therefore second-class citizens—a troubling and frustrating experience for expatriates) or as a new kind of social animal—almost as if they were from another planet.

Many female expatriates are treated with extreme politeness, but their professional input is ignored. Some find their "other" status increases their effectiveness. If an expatriate woman has a Ph.D., her chances of being effective increase dramatically, for in some ways she becomes an "honorary man."

Ironically, national women often work on development projects as support staff or junior professionals and may be treated with deference by expatriate males. National male staff usually treat female colleagues according to the norms of local social contexts, where women generally have little access to resources or power. Gender equity in staffing of development projects has become an issue as more women gain professional credentials and experience and as project leaders and donors realize the benefits of having women working professionally on these projects. Expatriate and national women are still on the fringe of development, but they have found common ground through discussions held during the UN Decade for Women (1976–1985).[12]

The continued male domination of international development in all professions is evidence that gender issues have generally been ignored.

Gender equity in staffing of development projects has become an issue as more women gain professional credentials and experience. A U.S. economist is shown here discussing research methodology with Vietnamese economists. (Photo by Sarah Tisch)

USAID and other donors have tried to remedy this through women in development (WID) programs and training in **gender sensitivity** (an approach that considers the presence of social, cultural, economic, and political inequalities or inequities that may exist between men and women) and **gender analysis** (a methodology that helps identify access to, and control over, productive resources, income sources, expenditures, and division of labor between men and women). Women are slowly achieving positions of authority in the international development community. Donors try to ensure gender balance on projects, but success has been mixed. There are few female heads of PVOs and NGOs; women in private consulting firms have made more progress, partly because some donors (such as USAID) give preference to proposals from minority- or female-owned consulting firms.

Many studies show that neglecting women's concerns in development issues leads to inefficient resource use, greater inequity, and projects that fail to achieve their goals.[13] One frequently mentioned constraint is the lack of women in government service and as development workers and professionals. This is important, because women are needed in field situations where cultural norms constrain village women from speaking freely with men who are not relatives.

Why are few women involved in key policymaking decisions in multilateral, bilateral, and PVO/NGO development organizations? This may result from the long-standing male orientation of states, based on patriarchal cultural structures, bureaucratic rules that enforce the status quo, and the bias of constituencies outside official state bureaucracies.[14] The private and nonprofit sectors depend on official state or donor funding for many of their activities, so it is not surprising to find more men than women working for these organizations.

Cynthia Enloe investigates women's participation in international relations by looking at support roles women traditionally occupy. Enloe contends that it is as "wife, mother, secretary, and sexy broad" that women have exerted influence over men and international relations, and she calls for an examination of these roles.[15]

Men and women must work together to achieve development goals. How should they define their roles and divide the tasks? Gender issues affect how development policies, programs, and projects are designed, funded, implemented, and evaluated. Projects that try to be gender sensitive can count the women included in training and given access to new technologies; it is more difficult to measure the impact of training and access to resources on women's control over productive resources. Questions must be asked about each woman:

- □ Has her work burden lessened or increased?
- □ What impact has her participation had on household production?
- □ Has her family benefited from her experience?
- □ What effect has the project had on her existing welfare networks?
- □ Most important, is the woman more empowered to control her destiny and use of resources than she was before the project began?

Are men or women better suited to work on WID problems or gender issues? Most women active in international development argue for training both the male and female staffs of public and private agencies in gender sensitivity and gender analysis, requiring gender balance among project staff, and requiring gender analysis of projects—beginning with proposals. The gender of individual development workers is less important than their sensitivity to gender issues. However, for balance, more women must be recruited into public and private development organizations.[16]

Equity between men and women is particularly difficult to achieve in donor-funded training. Unless special arrangements are made to reserve seats for women, most fellowship and participant training programs are dominated by males. For sociocultural reasons, women in developing countries are reluctant to compete with men for scarce training opportunities, a highly valued part of technology transfer. Communities and bureaucracies rarely promote women over men in the belief that men provide cash incomes for their families and, therefore, should have enhanced skills and training.

Other barriers to female involvement in training programs include cultural traditions that limit women's freedom to travel from their family homesteads alone, difficulties in providing child care while women are gone, and women's reluctance to leave their families—in part because of a lack of family support for them to improve their skills and change their status. Some development projects try to overcome these barriers by holding small, local trainings so women need not travel far, and some reserve space for women so they need not compete with men.

The Agricultural Research and Production Project in Nepal tried to find innovative ways to ensure female participation in training. Accommodations were arranged for women when training programs lasted more than one day. Tutors were hired to help women prepare for the junior technical assistant exam; all of the tutored women passed the exam. These women returned to their districts with temporary positions and were assisted in developing extension programs aimed at female farmers or programs for tasks women typically perform. Training was provided for 36 women to become agricultural assistants. Female farmers were trained alongside males in livestock extension, animal health, pastures and forages, routine animal health diagnosis, and general animal management. By understanding that trained, competent women at the village level were important for project success, government officials and project implementors found ways to increase female participation in the project's training programs.[17]

THE DEVELOPMENT COMMUNITY

Interaction among development professionals affects the design of development projects, and expatriate and national motivations influence project implementation. All stages of development assistance are affected by members of the larger development community in each country, which includes individuals from donor and recipient agencies, banks, implementing firms, and PVOs/NGOs—all of whom interact with each other on a national and international basis. The collective will of this community has a profound effect on how development projects are designed, implemented, and replicated.

The development community of expatriate advisers and elite, Ph.D.-trained developing country nationals forms what Ernst Haas calls an "epi-

The Agricultural Research and Production Project in Nepal tried to find innovative ways to ensure female participation in training; here, a Nepalese junior technical assistant with buffalo. (Photo by Jim Yazman, courtesy of Winrock International)

stemic community." These work communities have cultural standards and social arrangements that revolve around primary commitments to epistemic criteria in the production and application of knowledge. International organizations have standards of verification and rules of behavior that ultimately assure the truth of their findings.[18]

The knowledge generated within this community comprises the current wisdom on how countries can develop the most quickly with the fewest resources and the least upheaval in social relations. Consulting groups and nonprofit institutions charged with designing and implementing development projects compete with each other within this community for access to the resources that perpetuate the knowledge of development each implementing group professes to have. These resources, in turn, affect the ways projects are designed and implemented.

Epistemic communities are successful if they claim to have information that is more convincing to political decisionmakers than are other sources of knowledge.[19] International organizations—such as the World Bank, the International Monetary Fund, and the United Nations—have gained the confidence and experience to advise recipient governments on how to develop. These organizations claim they know how to stimulate development better than national governments themselves.[20] Thus, these international organizations have gained status as the "experts" on socioeconomic development.

New trends in development theory and implementation result from the competitive interaction of these group members on both national and international levels. Because this is an exclusive community—to join, one must have the requisite bureaucratic experience, education, international experience, and friendships—it is far removed from the people its projects purport to help. Ironically, the more cohesive professional development communities are, the less connection they tend to have with local communities. Discussions tend to take place within these professional communities rather than with the people they are trying to assist; the survival of development organizations is dependent on pleasing the immediate clients (donors or national governments) rather than on improving the lives of the eventual beneficiaries (villagers).

Development banks—the World Bank, Asian Development Bank, African Development Bank, and Inter-American Development Bank—are criticized for reifying their own development models because their staff members see themselves as the only experts who can design sustainable development projects. Perhaps this occurs because these organizations are well funded and can directly implement their project ideas. Contact with other development actors—such as NGOs—tends to be limited and conflictive, partly because the banks and NGOs use different development paradigms and partly because bank staff have difficulty accepting NGO personnel as professionals.

The development community has both formal and informal networks. The Society for International Development, the largest of such networks, holds annual international meetings and regularly publishes a newsletter. The societies of specific professions—such as economics—also have subgroups of individuals interested in development. There is an informal network of consultants (called the "old-boy" network by outsiders) who have worked for a variety of consulting organizations. A new, U.S.-based professional network—the Association for Women in Development—for expatriate and national women who have worked on women in development issues, is an attempt to create a parallel network for women.

In most Asian countries, a jogging club, the Hash House Harriers, serves as a social network for expatriates working in development and private business.[21] Many other expatriate social networks are also important because expatriates often do not fit into the societies in which they work. These networks ease transitions into new cultures for expatriate diplomatic and consultant families and provide information on how to work within local systems.

CONCLUSION

Few countries have developed without inputs or investment from people of other countries. Nationals and expatriates will likely continue to work together on developmental problems. However, assessments of technical competence in implementing development activities are often complicated by diverging donor and recipient views of development goals. Donors usually wish to control development activities, even though recipients can often implement these activities themselves. In patriarchal societies, men often wish to retain control of resources, even though women are key decisionmakers in village agriculture and natural resource management.

In the Nepalese program described at the beginning of this chapter, funding was provided for regional short-term training in agricultural and natural resource project management and evaluation. In discussions about a training program in the Philippines, the candidates nominated to participate in the program focused on two questions: How much is the per diem? and Can I stop in Hong Kong en route to or from the program? No one asked about the substance of the program.

These candidates were being practical, knowing they may have little chance to apply skills learned in the training program and that the trip was more a reward for past performance and encouragement for future performance than an opportunity to acquire new skills. Recipient government officials want to control access to these programs because they know who has performed in the past and which candidates they want to reward. These candidates may not be the people who are the most capable of acquiring and using new skills. Donors must accept the negative aspects of elite-focused human resource development along with its positive effects, and devote more resources to participatory development, if they want to reach poor people on a widespread basis.

The three dilemmas of development assistance—economic, political, and individual—are dynamic problems, changing as the nature of development evolves. In Chapter 5 we discuss the future of development by examining a range of current development issues.

FIVE

□   □   □

Does Development
Have a Future?

Fifteeen years after completing my Peace Corps assignment, I returned to the village in which I had been posted as a volunteer. The seasons have not changed, but the village has. Life is still hard for most villagers, but there are signs of progress—this village is developing, albeit slowly. How much has this village been affected by development assistance to Nepal since I left in the mid-1970s? Its physical circumstances have certainly changed.

The village hospital—a concrete building often unoccupied since its construction (I lived there for a year when there was no doctor)—now has a doctor with an Indian B.S. degree who is usually there. Infant and child mortality are still problems, but vaccinations are given to children when serum is available. Most of the doctor's work consists of prescribing medicines and dietary cures for villagers' ailments. For treatment of more serious problems, villagers must still travel far.

The most noticeable change in clothing is the shift toward Western clothes by the young village boys: T-shirts obtained from nearby markets, with various product brand names and slogans, are the preferred dress.

Land distribution is still skewed; so are income and wealth. The poor are somewhat better off, but the gap between rich and poor has probably widened.

More children—both boys and girls—attend school, and they stay in school longer. Two thatched classrooms have been built to supplement the concrete school building and to accommodate the additional students. There are two more teachers than there were before, but all teachers are still male.

The number of tractors has doubled, from three to six (the same families that owned the three own the six), and there are more bicycles. No one owns a passenger vehicle. There is electricity for a few hours some days, but still no telephone or running water. There is a rice mill run by a diesel engine.

The houses look the same, but there are more of them to accommodate the increased population.

Although more girls are going to school, traditional gender roles are barely changed. The young girls I used to see playing near their houses now hide behind closed doors—they are married women, and contact with unrelated males is taboo.

117

*Villagers are traveling more. A gravel road passes by the north side of the village,
connecting two district centers, and villagers take advantage of this road to conduct more
commerce within Nepal, although they still maintain personal and commercial relations
with Indians across the nearby border. More villagers have been to Kathmandu, some to
seek jobs from a man from the adjoining district who was for a time the minister of
agriculture.*

*This village is well situated to take advantage of development—it is located in the
plains, where transportation is easy. Its proximity to India provides it with information,
agricultural inputs, and consumer goods. It is on the road between two district centers, has
electricity, and caters to local travelers. The electricity, the road, and the hospital all exist
because of foreign assistance money.*

*Other villages in Nepal are less fortunate. Hill and mountain villages have less contact
with the outside world, but even in these regions air transport is making a difference.
Lightweight consumer goods from Hong Kong and Bangkok can be found even in remote
district centers in the mountains.*

*The number of Nepalis who have experience in other countries has increased; many
male mountain villagers have served with the Indian or British armies (in the famed
Gurkha regiments) and have returned with money, skills, and the motivation to improve
their lives. Others have traveled south (using roads in Nepal and an extensive
transportation system in India) for seasonal or semipermanent labor in India.*

*Nepalese villagers can take advantage of gains from trade, and improve their lives with
imported technology, more easily than they can improve their own production efficiency.
Unfortunately, Nepal has few exports with which to pay for imported goods. It has little
comparative advantage in foreign markets in any area except perhaps its inexpensive labor.
Official development assistance can pay for some imports, but the national debt is
increasing.*

*What does the future hold for Nepalese villages? What is likely to change villages—
infrastructure, economic production, or social behavior? What needs to change in villages,
and who can and should make and pay for these changes? What will happen as agricultural
technology begins to benefit wealthier farmers, widening income gaps in villages even as
welfare gains are made by poor farmers?*

*Expectations are rising, and a few individuals' sense of themselves as change agents in
their own lives is also increasing. Will these few be able to solve the increasingly complex
problems resulting from population growth, environmental degradation, and declining per
capita food production? What role will foreign development assistance play in helping
Nepal address these problems?*

Development aid no longer has the novelty it once did. In the 1950s
and 1960s, when the United States was first becoming formally involved in development activities, the challenge was to solve new problems. For the most part, those problems have been more difficult and more
frustrating than originally anticipated, and the glamour is gone. People

know what should work but somehow cannot make it happen. The remaining difficulties are mostly administrative and bureaucratic, and official development assistance may not be the key to solving these problems.

A NEW ERA FOR DEVELOPMENT AID

The ideological paradigm that served as a basis for development assistance, which was so important during the Cold War, has become largely irrelevant. During this period, aid allocations rose and fell according to the fortunes of the East-West conflict around the world. European donors and multilateral institutions were also deeply affected by the U.S.-USSR conflict.

Raymond Hopkins claims that two unique events have affected international relations since 1945: interdependent security arrangements in response to nuclear weapons and the transfer of resources from rich countries to poor in recognition of global economic interdependencies.[1] These two phenomena have shaped a development assistance regime based on institutionalized rules and practices, resource flows focused on developing countries, expansion of multilateral aid, growth of recipient country bargaining power, and economic development as the primary goal for development assistance.

Development assistance flows are altered when political, economic, and humanitarian concerns change. In 1991, for example, global politics changed dramatically with the dissolution of the Soviet Union. Bilateral aid has always been a function of specific political objectives, especially in solidifying political and economic relations between donor and recipient countries.

Although development assistance comprises its own regime,[2] it has also been used to encourage developing countries to participate in Western trade instead of pursuing self-sufficiency or adopting communism. Food aid has been an effective tool of bilateral assistance; it satisfies political goals while simultaneously feeding hungry people. Although there are many critiques of food aid, it continues to be valued by developing countries and to be useful to developed countries.[3]

The structure of the world system of states is changing rapidly. The sovereign state has not diminished in importance as was envisioned by planners of the UN system of multilateral institutions. Although sovereign states formally cooperate more than they ever have within the context of multilateral institutions, individual state interests are still critically important. Formal sovereignty and national interests are more important than they have ever been, and the number of new states entering the world system will continue to grow as people in Eastern Europe and the former USSR reidentify themselves. New states may also emerge in Africa as long-standing feuds over territory are resolved.

The increased needs of new states seeking development assistance have not been matched by proportional growth in donor funding. Japan is the only bilateral donor that has dramatically increased its development assistance budget during the past 20 years.[4] For other donors, some funds formerly reserved for developing countries have been reallocated to Eastern Europe and the former USSR.

This reallocation is partly a result of recognition of the fact that development assistance is needed by former centrally planned economies; it is also a result of the progress some countries have made. Some states have received enough socioeconomic investment to drastically reduce or eliminate their need for development assistance (Singapore, South Korea, and Taiwan are examples). Official development assistance to Latin America and most of Asia has been declining since the late 1960s; Africa is the only region whose share of ODA has increased since 1961.[5]

Bilateral funding reductions resulting from pressure on donor governments to use funds for domestic purposes has increased recipient reliance on multilateral institutions. There is pressure on multilateral institutions to use more flexible funding policies and instruments in the face of bilateral aid reductions. However, multilateral organizations are public institutions—they rely on regular contributions from member governments, and these contributions have not increased in proportion to the needs of new clients or the reductions in bilateral aid.

The roles and responsibilities of multilateral donors will be redefined as the post–Cold War world system becomes clear. Until the basis and justification for development assistance change, this new world system will depend on transfers from rich countries to poor. Transfers will still be based on political decisions made by individual donor states in the context of their contributions to multilateral agencies and bilateral programs. The distinction between bilateral and multilateral assistance will continue to erode as donor coordination increases and multiple donors focus on policy-related issues and projects for individual countries.[6]

Does official development assistance help achieve new visions of development, or does it hinder that vision? The moral basis for resource transfers from rich countries to poor was transparent in the aftermath of colonialism and in the heat of the Cold War ideological struggle. Citizens in donor countries and development aid professionals now question whether development assistance should continue if it benefits mainly the upper classes (trickle down) and corrupt government officials. Other bilateral donors wonder about the effectiveness of development aid in nondemocratic systems. As David C. Korten observes:

The development industry, created during the past four decades to respond to a global commitment to alleviating poverty, is in a state of disarray. The landscape is littered with evidence of failures of official development efforts to reach the poor. The largest of the multilateral and bilateral assistance agencies have responded to the failure by focusing once again on accelerating economic growth. They argue if adequate growth rates can be sustained, the poor will be swept along with the tide of rising incomes. The argument is reassuring but reflects more a hopeful myth than a pragmatic reality.[7]

What does the future hold for development definitions, for the economics and politics of development, and for individuals? Expatriate and national development practitioners have long advocated a more long-term, holistic view of development assistance. In the remainder of this chapter we discuss the future of the Western model of development assistance, examine ethics and equity issues, and assess the future of foreign development assistance.

THE WESTERN MODEL
OF DEVELOPMENT ASSISTANCE

The predominant model of development assistance—the "Western" model—has long been under scrutiny and criticism from many fronts.[8] Despite its shortcomings, the model remains the predominant mode for bilateral and multilateral development assistance. The new realities of the world system of states and the formation of a new world order may result in other models being tried, but none has yet gained the confidence of major donors.

The Western model is characterized by funding from donors extended on a project basis and managed by expatriate professionals. Projects are designed, implemented, and evaluated primarily by donors, with some input from recipient governments. Expatriates, rather than local professionals, are usually hired for project implementation and administration because there are too few qualified local experts, it is believed that outsiders can encourage change more effectively than nationals, and it is easier for donors to control project funds. The Western model has a short time horizon—development assistance is designed to "prime the pump," initiating growth that is ultimately intended to be self-sustaining.

Ethics Issues

The Western model of development assistance is based on a functional perspective, postulating that if economic growth is stimulated by official development assistance, the inequities and injustices supported by undeveloped economies will be reduced. The number of people living in poverty will decrease, the basic needs of citizens will be met, markets will expand, economic opportunities will increase, and governments will respond to the economic and political needs of their people. Socioeconomic development occurs in an environment of economic growth. The role of official development assistance is to stimulate economic growth, build infrastructure, and provide information, technology, and training to country nationals. Eventually progress will be sufficient to reduce the need for development assistance.

Critics from developing and developed countries have faulted the Western model precisely because this functional perspective lacks an ethical framework that addresses the core causes of underdevelopment and poverty.[9] The rapid changes designed to stimulate economic growth—improvements in agricultural technology, macroeconomic policy change, trade and industrial expansion, and infrastructure creation—have far-reaching effects on social structure. Unfortunately, there are often unintended negative consequences, such as those experienced through structural adjustment programs.

Structural adjustment programs, which depend on macroeconomic policy reform by recipient governments, have emerged as blueprints for developing countries to achieve financial stability. These programs attempt to improve countries' balances of payments so currencies are valued at market rates; it is assumed that liberalizing trade and lifting investment restrictions will eliminate inefficiencies and raise living standards. National financial stability is seen as the foundation for sustained economic growth and development. Most of these programs are relatively recent innovations, so their long-term impact remains to be seen.

The IMF and the World Bank jointly implement structural adjustment programs with recipient governments. The IMF designs programs and supplies advice, and the World Bank provides structural adjustment loans. Such programs usually require devaluing currency, reducing public spending, ending food subsidies, and reducing trade and investment restrictions. The schedule for compliance with adjustment targets is usually three to five years, but developing countries often need more time.

The short-term effects of structural adjustment programs are often devastating for recipient governments and poor people. Recipient governments have experienced food riots and domestic political instability following the implementation of these programs. These governments lose control of domestic economic decisions, and poor people lose the benefit of government-funded social programs. Reductions in food subsidies, low-cost medical care, free education, and access to credit dramatically limit the ability of urban and rural poor people to care for their families.[10]

Program implementation has led to questions concerning the morality of structural adjustment. Why should poor people suffer as a result of government inefficiency and failed macroeconomic policies?

Acceptance of structural adjustment programs has become an economic "clean bill of health" for developing countries. Widespread bilateral and multilateral donor involvement in structural adjustment negotiations has created an informal norm that is now accepted by donors: Structural adjustment programs assure donors that aid money will be spent rationally. Whether structural adjustment will lead to higher standards of living and greater long-term employment opportunities for the poor is yet unknown. In the short run, the PVO and NGO sector is helping those hit hardest by cuts in government programs.

The development of appropriate technology provides another important example of unintended consequences of the Western model. Green Revolution technology (high-yielding seed varieties for major cereal crops—rice, maize, and wheat—that depend on irrigation, chemical fertilizer, and pesticide use) has been developed primarily at the donor-supported international agricultural research centers. These centers were created to help increase world food supplies, thus reducing the need for food aid and eliminating hunger as the primary problem for human society. Green Revolution technologies were intended to increase agricultural productivity and raise farmers' incomes while stimulating growth in other sectors. Although the impact of these technologies is still being assessed, the initial beneficiaries have clearly been wealthier farmers with access to irrigation.[11] In addition, declining agricultural yields in many places raise new questions concerning the impact of these technologies on reducing poverty.[12]

Finally, economic change rarely occurs without concomitant social and cultural changes. Development assistance is explicitly designed to support economic change, and recipient countries may not want the associated cultural change. However, cultural change may be necessary in order for countries to develop; development is as much about personal and social values as it is about incomes, life expectancy, and literacy rates. The impact of Western society—transmitted mostly by global communications technology but also through the values and life-styles of Western development professionals—on traditional societies seldom results in equitable social structures.[13] With the inequities and violence now found in developed economies, it is difficult to give developing countries attractive examples of social models to emulate.[14]

Externally funded development also raises issues of **cultural imperialism**. Few places in the world have not been touched by Western advertising, media, or consumer goods. The presence of expatriates and development projects often raises expectations, especially among young people. Values are constantly changing (if slowly); new technologies and foreign aid abet these value changes. Cultural imperialism occurs when one society imposes its values on another; ideally, development activities provide information and resources and allow individuals to make free choices. However, as more incentives (resources) are provided to entice people to change their values, the charge of cultural imperialism may continue.

There is growing concern over the lack of explicit ethics in development project formulation and implementation. Overall, development economics has not directly confronted moral issues; the work of Amartya Sen is a notable exception.[15] Incorporating ethical principles into economic models that predict the impact of technologies or policies on economic growth would be an important step forward.[16]

The objective of addressing ethical issues is to understand how political and economic factors perpetuate injustice and how injustice sustains poverty.[17] Without this understanding, it is difficult to assess the impact of specific projects on reducing or perpetuating poverty. Development assistance is often blamed as a key factor in the widening gap between rich and poor; however, in view of the low levels of official development assistance to most developing countries, it is difficult to place the blame entirely on aid.[18] Many mistakes have been made, and development assistance has been hampered by the political concerns of donor governments and elites in recipient countries. The problems of underdevelopment and poverty require an analysis of equity as well as ethics.

Equity Issues

What accounts for the differences between rich and poor? How much is the result of the luck of birth, and how much is the product of personal effort? Most developing countries lack the extensive physical infrastructure, such as transportation and communication networks, that facilitates personal mobility. In rural societies, those born near roads are lucky. Some people born far from roads will overcome this disadvantage and become relatively well-off, but most will have lower standards of living than their more fortunate fellow citizens who are born near roads.

It seems, from humans' limited ability to perceive and distinguish such influences, that men's and women's lives are influenced by both luck and effort, by both nature and nurture. Positive attitudes help, but initial circumstances also matter. Attitudes that would be sufficient to make someone wealthy in favorable circumstances may make only a small difference in unfavorable conditions and leave the person frustrated in the bargain.

With few exceptions—usually the results of concentrated political and economic resources, which cannot be widely replicated—economic variables change slowly. Reducing population growth, increasing food production, and improving environmental quality all take time. It is unrealistic to expect that countries with average per capita incomes of less than $300 will be able to multiply these tenfold in 10, 20, or even 50 years. Per capita GNP rarely grows at a rate of more than 5 percent per year for more than a few years at a time. To bring the 24 countries with average per capita incomes of less than $300 up to $3,000 would require 25 years of 10 percent annual growth.[19]

Even if growth in per capita incomes is achieved, the distribution of wealth is likely to remain a problem. The experience with food production illustrates the possibility of achieving an average target and failing to meet the needs of more than half the population of many countries. Developing countries now have enough food to feed themselves (average daily per capita supplies equal 2,440 calories, well above subsistence needs of about 2,000 calories), yet 21 countries meet less than 90 percent of their own food requirements, and 27 import more than 50 percent of their food.[20]

Distribution (equity) will be an increasingly important issue in development; focusing on equity requires an ethical perspective. Establishing this ethical perspective must involve all stakeholders in the development process—donors, recipient governments, public and private development practitioners, for-profit and nonprofit organizations, communities and individuals. Despite internationally voiced humanitarian concerns, countries do not yet share values concerning access to resources, technology, and capital. No consensus exists on how much development aid should be extended from rich to poor, for how long, in what mode (grant or loan), or on who should control the distribution and use of aid.

A CHANGING MODEL

Western development theory—with its model of economic growth and its implementing mechanism of official development assistance—assumes that the process of development does not lead to irreconcilable differences among people; that there are no structural barriers to development with respect to terms of trade, financial flows, technology development, copyright issues, and market opportunities; that traditional practices inhibit growth and efficiency; and that development inevitably leads to Western-style modernization. Dependency theory refutes these positions, claiming that traditional and modern values depend on context and that the Western model of development assistance is not easily adapted to non-Western cultural and social contexts.

Jan K. Black claims the Western model is replete with paradoxes that make both implementing projects and achieving positive results for the poor difficult.[21] Because of these paradoxes, critics from developing countries are reassessing the meaning of development. Some of the new criteria suggested to redefine development include the existence of market economies, concern for human rights, gender equity, environmental protection, participatory local management of resources, local democratic forms of decisionmaking, and economic self-sufficiency.[22] The emphasis on local management and bottom-up development has long been advocated; it is now gaining more credence from both donor and recipient governments.[23]

However, perhaps because of its many critics, this model is slowly changing.[24] More nationals are now leading and managing donor-funded projects as a result of the growing expertise of local professionals who have both university educations and experience outside their own countries. In part this is the fruit of human resource training and development programs. There is a growing recognition that sustainable long-term changes are best initiated and nurtured by people who are citizens of developing countries. Expatriates are also extremely expensive, and their cost—often over $200,000 per year per expert, including travel and housing—is difficult to justify if local expertise is available.

Nongovernmental organizations are increasingly capable of designing and implementing effective projects. NGOs provide sustainable project implementation as a result of their local perspective, use of participatory approaches, need to retain local legitimacy, and long-term commitment to specific areas or problems.[25] As a result, some donors are increasing their funding for NGOs.

Although donors are still reluctant to view NGOs as full partners in the development process, there appears to be a slow shift in the development paradigm, with donors including NGOs in more policy and issues consultations. However, some national governments feel threatened by NGOs, and there is a need for expanded discussion about their roles in the design, implementation, and evaluation of projects.

As long as official development assistance follows the Western model, governments will continue to be the chief recipients of funds, expertise, and goods. The extent to which these are effectively utilized to benefit poor people depends upon the objectives and abilities of recipient governments. It is in this area that NGOs can help recipient governments and make a tremendous difference in implementing the model.

National for-profit firms have also gained donor confidence in their capabilities to carry out development activities and deliver results. Expatriate firms that obtain contracts with donor agencies often subcontract with local firms to provide professional expertise to implement projects.

Recipient states are increasing their bargaining power in controlling the nature of projects, influencing the selection of contractors, and deciding who administers project funds. A partnership model—working in collaboration with recipient states instead of using the more paternalistic Western model—is gaining more currency.[26] This approach calls for reducing the dominance of donors in project design, implementation, and evaluation.

Developing countries want more control over development aid. With the decline of aid used for ideological competition between the West and

Communist states, this demand will grow. Donors and recipients will continue to struggle with issues of control regarding who can better appreciate priorities, resources, and potentials.[27]

Two economists, Uma Lele and Ijaz Nabi, offer a penetrating assessment of the Western model by examining the effectiveness of official development assistance and external financing in 11 developing countries. Their conclusions are drawn from lessons learned about the Western model of development since World War II.[28]

Lele and Nabi conclude that although development assistance is not the most important element in development, it can assist governments committed to growth-oriented economic policies. Other findings include:

- External capital is not a substitute for fiscal reform and domestic resource mobilization.
- Political commitment is essential for responsible macroeconomic management and policy reform.
- Aid can help cushion painful adjustments.
- Promoting outward-oriented policies with external financing stimulates rapid GDP growth and employment.
- Agricultural productivity is key to improving overall economic performance.
- Food aid programs help protect poor and vulnerable groups while programs are implemented to increase domestic production.
- Growth and equity depend on investment in human capital.
- Programs for women in development and the environment benefit from external financial and technical assistance.[29]

Although these findings should not surprise experienced development practitioners, they reaffirm the positive role aid can play and indicate the specific contexts in which aid can be most effective. These conclusions reaffirm the need for commitment on the part of developing countries: Aid can only help countries; it cannot force development in the absence of the political will necessary to make changes. They provide an empirical basis for further refining the theory of development and for improving the effectiveness of development activities.

For development donors, Lele and Nabi's analysis provides both encouragement and warnings:

- Aid can harm a country if serious policy distortions and imbalances exist.
- Supporting policy reform in richer developing countries improves access to commercial capital markets, promotes growth, and releases resources for less-developed countries.

□ Aid programs help encourage private-sector involvement in development.
□ Successful aid depends on stable and predictable donor efforts.
□ Long-term development consequences of aid must be considered.
□ External financing can encourage poverty alleviation policies.
□ Humanitarian aid is necessary for the least-developed countries, even if policies are distorted.
□ Donors should avoid rapid changes in sector focus and fads.
□ Donor coordination results in better aid programs.
□ Aid tying in bilateral programs uses resources suboptimally.
□ In the long run, sustainable capital and technology transfers from developed to developing countries are best achieved through trade rather than aid.[30]

Although it stops short of recommending ethical principles for development assistance, Lele and Nabi's analysis summarizes experience with the Western model. Although serious consideration of the lessons Lele and Nabi describe could significantly affect the distribution of development assistance, as well as project design and implementation, these lessons are not usually incorporated into structural adjustment programs. These conclusions—based on the past practice of development assistance—could also lay the foundation for future alternative models. Unfortunately, Lele and Nabi do not address the powerful role NGOs can play as equal development partners with donors and governments.

Despite trends toward modifying the Western model, this model is still the primary mode of foreign development assistance. Recent evidence of the challenges confronting the model arose during the 1992 UN Conference on the Environment and Development (UNCED) in Brazil. Parallel meetings (the Global Forum) were held among NGOs, citizen groups, people's organizations, and activists. Although UNCED produced agreement on two major treaties addressing biodiversity and climatic change, tensions arose among participants in UNCED and the Global Forum over the role of development assistance, appropriate models for development, and responsibility for protecting the environment and alleviating poverty.

THE FUTURE OF
FOREIGN DEVELOPMENT ASSISTANCE

Definitions

What will change the current definitions of development, and how will new definitions be reflected in development assistance? Equity and sustainability are receiving increasing attention with the realization that resources are finite and must be protected and distributed through collaborative action. Changing definitions may result from statistics that more accurately portray the complex and diverse relations among income and other key dimensions of development.[31] These relations are complex within each country, and they are diverse across countries. Increasing evidence of this complexity and diversity will diminish the focus on income as the main indicator of development.

The emphasis on income will decline in favor of definitions that focus on health and education, which will likely be defined in terms of life expectancy and literacy. These indicators do not change as rapidly—nor are they measured as often—as incomes, which can fluctuate widely with changes in weather, economic cycles, and political alliances. This should lead to an increasing realization that development is often a slow process.

There may be no unique way to capture the distribution of development measures, such as per capita income, life expectancy, or literacy. The increasing recognition that improving distribution within a country is as important as raising average values, however, will ensure that equity considerations play a significant role in defining development goals.

As with equity, there is no simple way to define or measure sustainability. Improved natural resources accounting (which measures the environmental costs of resource depletion) will help, but this technique is in its infancy, even in industrial countries. However, even without precise measurements, the concept of sustainability has been accepted by developed and developing countries, thus promoting increasing concern and encouraging continued efforts to refine quantitative measures.

The definition of sustainability will continue to be debated, with arguments ranging from concern for technical and economic criteria to ecological standards to community responsibility for maintaining sustainable resource bases.[32] Intergenerational needs for sustainability cannot be ignored, but much debate will focus on how to use resources for today's needs while ensuring that future generations will also be able to use productive resources.[33]

The definition of development will change as people and cultures change. The next decade will have different priorities from the current one, and the next generation's preferences may be inconceivable today. Although the basic dimensions of human development—income, health, education—may not change quickly, the practical expressions of these dimensions may. As incomes rise, leisure time becomes more important than acquiring more income; as life expectancy increases, comfort in old age becomes more important than achieving longer life; as literacy increases, diversity in education becomes more important than attaining greater literacy. Unfortunately, most countries are a long way from facing these tradeoffs for more than a small fraction of their populations.

On a more mundane level, there are obvious changes. In health, AIDS—a problem that was unknown 25 years ago—now threatens the entire populations of several African countries and is changing the social fabric of both developing and developed countries. The ability to determine the sex of unborn children, coupled with modern abortion techniques, is significantly altering the sex ratios of the populations of several developing countries, notably, China and India.[34] Although the populations of most developed countries are aging, those of many developing countries are getting younger as infant mortality declines and birth rates do not. In education, computers are creating opportunities for unprecedented advances in living standards and increasing the gaps between those who are skilled and those who are not.

As more information becomes available and conditions change, people will construct new indices of environmental and political development. These will serve to highlight the diversity of conditions among the countries of the world and contribute to the design of better programs and projects by donors and recipient governments. How these definitions mesh with official development assistance will depend on the relations among donors, recipient states, and other partners in the development process.

Development Models

Governments of rich and poor countries are being forced by their own constituents to consider equity and sustainability in foreign development assistance. The lessons of past failures and successes make prescriptions more obvious, but these must be adapted to constantly changing circumstances.

For donors and development practitioners, recognition of the complexity and diversity of development processes is redirecting the search for explanatory, and often quantitative, theories of development toward the documentation of case studies illustrating lessons learned from the experiences of various project strategies in different economic, political, and cultural situations. Governments and donors must be willing to learn from the past and from the local people involved in or affected by development projects.

Trickle-down theories, both social (help rich people and poor people will follow) and individual (increase personal incomes and improvements in other living standards will follow), will continue to be replaced by theories that directly address the needs of poor people and that focus explicitly on health, education, environmental, and political variables.

The Western model of donor-funded development projects will probably not radically change local social structures and empower the poor. However, projects incorporating participatory approaches may help to

Government and donors must be willing to learn from the past and from the local people, such as these Indian farmers, involved in or affected by development projects. (Photo by Jim Yazman, courtesy of Winrock International)

create conditions conducive for change. Local people will make dramatic social changes if such changes help to meet local needs. Governments sometimes impose change on people, but these efforts usually fail unless the government enjoys a high degree of legitimacy among its citizens. The rise of NGOs as key social actors can help to facilitate positive changes.

There will be increasing focus on the physical environment and political rights. The environment is important for the present because it affects human health through air and water quality; it is important for the future because it affects the natural resource base on which food production depends. Political rights are important both as ends in themselves and because they affect socioeconomic status. As these issues gain more currency in official development assistance negotiations, they will have a lasting impact on the evolution of the Western model.

Donor-Recipient Relations

Rich and poor countries will continue to prefer development assistance as a means to transmit wealth, information, and technology from rich to poor countries. Wealthy countries will continue to be both bilateral and multilateral donors as long as protecting their positions in the world community remains important. Recipient countries will continue to struggle with donor influence and control of policy and implementation issues.

Most donor states continue to debate the usefulness of official bilateral and multilateral assistance. Few countries provide the agreed-upon target mentioned earlier of 0.7 percent of their GNP for development aid.[35] Short-term project results—which are rarely dramatic—often do not convince donor legislatures, which are confronted with pressing domestic problems, to raise aid levels. The long-term links between rich and poor countries' standards of living are still not considered important by many people in developed countries.

The connections among economic growth, environmental protection, population control, and sustainable agricultural production are inescapable. Countries are too interdependent today to ignore differences in wealth and resource consumption levels. However, donors—frustrated by slow progress, corruption, and bureaucratic malaise in poor countries—are looking toward market solutions rather than aid to stimulate economic growth. Although the spectacular growth in East Asia is often cited as an example of how the market can work, these countries previously had considerable infrastructure and substantial domestic and foreign investment. Missing from the analogy are the roles played by aid, foreign investment, control of corruption, ethnic equity, political stability, information technology, and the use of policy analysis in stimulating these economies, as well as the ability and willingness of nationals to invest in their own countries.[36]

Multilateral development organizations will continue to play critical roles in development, especially as donor countries—influenced by domestic politics—reduce bilateral aid. The World Bank and the regional development banks will improve their effectiveness if they increase grant funding for technical assistance and work with international and national PVOs and NGOs. The extent to which, and for what purposes, multilateral development assistance is tied to the political interests of individual countries will depend on the nature of the emerging post–Cold War world system.

Development Assistance Implementors

Increasing numbers of technically trained host country professionals diminish the need for foreign technical experts. Anticipating and articulating host country needs are continual problems for both host country officials and donor agency staff members. However, the managerial skills of expatriates are likely to continue to be in demand in the near future.

Less money will be available for human resource development training. Donors want national governments to take responsibility for formal and nonformal education efforts. NGOs working in villages are leading the way in using participatory approaches as models of human resource development. Donors are following this lead, supported by scientists who became frustrated with the poor adaptation of technologies that were channeled through official institutions. However, the need for field-sensitive scientists and managers remains.

Although there is increased emphasis on broad, long-term programs rather than narrow, short-term projects, most individuals involved in development are constrained by short time horizons. Expatriate experts, even those dubbed "long term," seldom stay in one country longer than five years; this is too short a time to see the results of most efforts. Individuals focus on the personal rewards of their own careers, not on the long-term impacts of those careers. Expatriates can support change and share skills for short periods, but nationals must decide which expatriate activities deserve continuation and replication.

Developing country national professionals will have increased responsibility for project design and implementation and for their own successes and failures. Recipient government officials will become more accountable as societies become more open and democratic, whereas those in the private sector will become more responsive to local and international development markets, competing with firms from developed countries for contracts. Partnerships and subcontracts with firms from developed countries will expand, with each side exploiting its own comparative advantage.

What lies ahead for villagers? Will the combined efforts of development organizations and individuals keep pace with the increasing complexity of development problems, particularly in the face of the world's growing population? Education efforts require generations unless fiscally strained national governments make massive commitments. Experience with participatory research that links male and female farmers with scientists has proven that this is an effective and rewarding approach for both parties and that it reduces farmer dependence on ineffective government extension efforts. The result empowers people to manage their own destinies and to take advantage of changing market forces. All individuals—expatriates, national professionals, and villagers—need the freedom to grow, to fail, and to learn to manage the future in the best way we can.[37]

CONCLUSION

In this book we examine three dilemmas in international externally funded development. Many factors that affect how and why countries develop have been omitted. Religion has long been a dominant influence on human life, and it is unlikely to disappear. People need to explain the unknown, and religion provides explanations of why the world appears as it

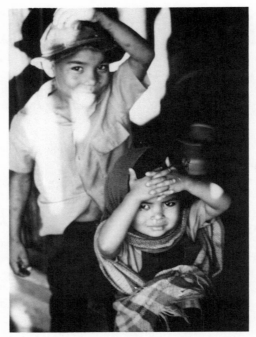

All individuals—expatriates, national professionals, and villagers, such as these Nepalese children—need the freedom to grow, to fail, and to
learn to manage the future. (Photo by Melissa
Yazman, courtesy of Winrock International)

does, why misfortune strikes good people, and why inequalities persist,
as well as offering hope for the future. This positive side of religion is balanced, and too often outweighed, by its tendency to divide populations
into believers and nonbelievers and to promote communal strife to
achieve the secular aims of religious leaders. It can also make people suspicious of change and susceptible to fatalistic explanations for human action. Depending upon how it is practiced, religion can thus play a positive
or negative role in the development process.

Although there has been a growing interest in Eastern philosophy in
the West, Western life-styles are a much greater influence on life in the
East, in both the North (Eastern Europe and the former Soviet Union) and
the South (the Third World). The influence of Western civilization will
likely increase because people want the material goods and services Western capitalist societies have provided for themselves—sometimes at the
expense of other societies or of other domestic values that have been recognized belatedly, such as the environment.

The basis for development assistance remains: Great differences exist in living standards between rich and poor countries, and the global community cannot afford to lose its members to hunger. Although the political justifications for development assistance changed with the end of the Cold War, defense budgets remain large, and the expected peace dividend in many wealthy countries has not been translated into more funds for development assistance to poor countries. Unfortunately, without massive resource transfers from rich to poor countries, coupled with stronger efforts to ensure that these transfers reach, benefit, and empower poor people, the world will continue to have far more hungry people than those who are well fed.

Fortunately, enough development assistance successes have occurred to encourage future efforts. However, there have also been enough failures to provide examples of directions to avoid and to promote realistic expectations for change. Optimism can prevail if the lessons of both successes and failures are learned and used by both donor and recipient governments, as well as by expatriate development practitioners, national professionals, and local villagers.

□   □   □

Discussion Questions

CHAPTER ONE

1. Is socioeconomic development higher incomes for more people? The production of more goods and services? Does it include better health—less disease and longer lives? What about education—basic reading and writing skills and opportunities for advanced training? Should the environment be included—air and water quality?

2. How should literacy be defined—as being able to write one's own name? Should years of schooling be included as a measure of education? How should primary and secondary schooling be compared? Should health be measured by life expectancy, infant and child mortality, or by weight-for-age standards and the incidence of disease?

3. Is it better to help a poor democratic country such as Mexico or the Philippines or an even poorer monarchy or dictatorship such as Bhutan or Zaire? Is it more important to assist flood victims in Bangladesh or war refugees in Iraq?

4. Is it better to implement projects quickly using expatriate technical assistance or more slowly with local professional skills and participation?

CHAPTER TWO

1. What are the most important dimensions of development?

2. How should these dimensions be measured?

3. Would you trade places with a villager in Asia, Africa, or Latin America? Why or why not? What would you gain and lose in such a trade?

4. Who decides what the definition of development will be? Who should decide?

5. Which has a greater long-term impact—improved seeds and chemical fertilizer, the values exemplified by the way the PCV lived, or the values by which the villagers lived (impact on the PCV)? Is changing technology more important than changing attitudes?

CHAPTER THREE

1. Do international organizations threaten state sovereignty?

2. What motivations should bilateral donors have for providing development assistance?

3. Is state sovereignty threatened by development aid?

4. Which contributes more to international stability, bilateral or multilateral development aid?

5. How much influence should donors have over domestic policy in poor countries?

CHAPTER FOUR

1. What role should public-sector and private-sector organizations play in the design and implementation of development projects?

2. How should donors and recipients choose among expatriates, national professionals, and potential beneficiaries in deciding who will design and implement development activities?

3. How should gender issues be integrated into development activities in male-dominated societies?

4. Should the salaries of expatriates and nationals be the same?

5. With which nationals should donors work—elites, the often small middle class, or disadvantaged ethnic groups? Should donor-funded development projects attempt to break down sociocultural barriers among these groups? Should these projects employ women in professional positions when they are not otherwise well represented on the staffs of national bureaucracies?

CHAPTER FIVE

1. Should reducing foreign aid be a long-term goal of donor countries? Or should more aid be provided to fewer countries to help alleviate the worst poverty?

2. How should donor and recipient countries work together to enhance environmental protection? Should environmental concerns override needs for economic growth in developing countries?

3. What kinds of foreign development assistance organizations should exist in the next century?

□ □ □

Notes

CHAPTER ONE

1. In this book, the terms *country, nation,* and *state* are used interchangeably for readability and convenience. Technically, a country is a geographic territory with definite borders recognized by its inhabitants. A nation is a group of people with a common sense of identity, a shared history and culture. A state is the legal entity that claims authority over a geographic territory; states control police and military forces, are recognized as rightful ruling entities by citizens, and are granted legal and diplomatic recognition by other states. A government is the bureaucratic apparatus of a state.

2. Programs are development activities designed to promote the achievement of general long-term objectives. Projects are development activities designed to achieve specific short-term objectives. Policies are statements of objectives and the general procedures for attaining these objectives.

CHAPTER TWO

1. The classic studies of the theory and history of economic growth are W. Arthur Lewis's *Theory of Economic Growth* (London: Unwin, 1955) and Simon Kuznets's *Modern Economic Growth: Rate, Structure and Spread* (New Haven, Conn.: Yale University Press, 1966). Kuznets's findings are summarized in "Modern Economic Growth: Findings and Reflections," *American Economic Review* 63, no. 3 (1973):247–258. For a critique of the relevance of history to developing countries, see Gunnar Myrdal, *The Challenge of World Poverty* (New York: Pantheon, 1970). More recent treatments include Michael P. Todaro, *Economic Development in the Third World* (New York: Longman, 1981), and Malcolm Gillis, Dwight H. Perkins, Michael Roemer, and Donald R. Snodgrass, *Economics of Development* (New York: W. W. Norton, 1983).

2. The *Human Development Report 1992* includes information on 160 countries; these are divided into 127 developing and 33 industrial countries. See United Nations Development Programme (UNDP), *Human Development Report 1992* (New York: Oxford University Press, 1992). The *World Development Report 1992* includes information on 125 countries that have populations of more than 1 million and provides basic indicators for 60 other economies. See World Bank, *World Development Report 1992* (New York: Oxford University Press, 1992).

3. UNDP, *Human Development Report 1992*, 98–100. Average per capita GNP in Switzerland in 1989 was $29,880; average per capita GNPs in 8 Asian and 16 African countries were $290 or less.

4. Ibid.

5. Ibid., 127–129. Life expectancy, the average length of life in a particular country, is the number of years a newborn infant could expect to live if prevailing patterns of mortality at the time of its birth were to stay the same throughout its life. Literacy is the ability to read and write. The adult literacy rate is the percentage of persons age 15 and over who can, with understanding, both read and write a short, simple statement on everyday life.

6. Ibid., 170–171, 202.

7. UNDP, *Human Development Report 1991* (New York: Oxford University Press, 1991), 161.

8. Todaro, *Economic Development in the Third World*, 531.

9. UNDP, *Human Development Report 1991*, 195.

10. UNDP, *Human Development Report 1992*, 98–100, 127–129.

11. Frances M. Lappe, Joseph Collins, and David Kinley, *Aid as an Obstacle: Twenty Questions About Our Foreign Aid and the Hungry* (San Francisco: Institute for Food and Development Policy, 1980), 81.

12. The 1990, 1991, and 1992 HDI used life expectancy to measure health. The 1990 HDI used the percentage of adult literacy to measure education. The 1991 and 1992 HDI combined adult literacy with mean years of schooling:

$$\text{education} = (2/3) \text{ literacy} + (1/3) \text{ years of schooling}$$

The 1990 HDI was based on the premise of diminishing returns from income to human development, using the logarithm of income and giving a zero weight to income above the poverty line (y^*):

$$W(y) = \log y \text{ for } 0 < y \leq y^*; \ W(y) = \log y^* \text{ for } y^* < y$$

The 1991 and 1992 HDI used an explicit formulation for diminishing returns, based on the Atkinson formulation for the utility of income:

$$W(y) = y \text{ for } 0 \leq y \leq y^* \text{ (the poverty line)}$$
$$W(y) = y^* + 2(y - y^*)^{1/2} \text{ for } y^* \leq y \leq 2y^*$$
$$W(y) = y^* + 2(y^*)^{1/2} + 3(y - 2y^*)^{1/3} \text{ for } 2y^* \leq y \leq 3y^* \text{ and so on}$$

The HDI measures income by real GDP per capita (purchasing power parities), developed by the United Nations International Comparison Project. Using this measure, in 1989 107 countries had average per capita incomes below the poverty line (y^*) of $4,829; 23 countries were between y^* and $2y^*$ ($4,829 and 9,658, respectively); 16 countries were between $2y^*$ and $3y^*$ ($9,658 and 14,487, respectively) ; 12 countries were between $3y^*$ and $4y^*$ ($14,487 and 19,316, respectively); and only 2 countries (the United States and the United Arab Emirates) were above $4y^*$ ($19,316).

13. UNDP, *Human Development Report 1992*, 127–131.

14. Ibid., 127–129.

15. Ibid., 127–131.

16. Michael Lipton with Richard Longhurst, *New Seeds for Poor People* (Baltimore: Johns Hopkins University Press, 1989).

17. Wolf Ladejinsky, "The Green Revolution in Punjab," *Agricultural Development Council Reprint No. 28* (New York: Agricultural Development Council, 1976).

18. See Todaro, *Economic Development in the Third World,* especially Chapter 3, for a discussion of development and income distribution.

19. UNDP, *Human Development Report 1991,* 152–153, 186.

20. UNDP, *Human Development Report 1992,* 92–93.

21. Ibid., 136–137.

22. See Todaro, *Economic Development in the Third World,* 64–67; Hans Singer, "Dualism Revisited: A New Approach to the Problems of Dual Society in Developing Countries," *Journal of Development Studies* 7, no. 1 (1970):60–61.

23. UNDP, *Human Development Report 1992,* 146–147.

24. See Daniel B. Schirmer and Stephen R. Shalom, *The Philippines Reader: A History of Colonialism, Neocolonialism, Dictatorship, and Resistance* (Boston: South End Press, 1987), 107, 193–204, 391; David Wurfel, *Filipino Politics: Development and Decay* (Ithaca, N.Y.: Cornell University Press, 1988), 24–37, 154–165, 176.

25. Roger East, ed., *Keesing's Record of World Events,* vol. 36 (Cambridge: Longman, 1990):37236, 37450, 37849.

26. Adam Smith, *An Inquiry into the Nature and Causes of the Wealth of Nations* (New York: Modern Library, 1937; orig. pub. 1776).

27. See Walter Rostow, *The Stages of Economic Growth* (London: Cambridge University Press, 1960).

28. See Todaro, *Economic Development in the Third World.*

29. UNDP, *Human Development Report 1992,* 164–165, 174–175.

30. Hollis Chenery and Moises Syrquin, *Patterns of Development, 1950–1970* (New York: Oxford University Press, 1975).

31. See World Bank, *World Development Report 1992,* 222–223; UNDP, *Human Development Report 1992,* 127–129.

32. See J. N. Bhagwati, *Foreign Trade Regimes and Economic Development: Anatomy and Consequences* (Cambridge, Mass.: Ballinger Publishing Co., 1978); Y. Hayami and V. W. Ruttan, *Agricultural Development: An International Perspective* (Baltimore: Johns Hopkins University Press, 1985); J. L. Lewis and V. Kallab, *Development Strategies Reconsidered* (New Brunswick, N.J.: Transaction Books, 1986); Randall B. Purcell and Elizabeth Morrison, *U.S. Agriculture and the Third World: The Critical Linkage* (Boulder, Colo.: Lynne Rienner Publishers, 1987); Romeo M. Bautista, "Price and Trade Policies for Agricultural Development," *The World Economy* 13, no. 1 (March 1990):89–109.

33. The International Agricultural Research Centers of the Consultative Group on International Agricultural Research (CGIAR) include 18 centers concerned with rice, maize, wheat, potatoes, vegetables, bananas and plantains, genetic resources, tropical agriculture, semiarid agriculture, dryland agriculture, irrigation, aquatic resources, livestock, animal diseases, food policy, and agroforestry.

34. See Daniel Lerner, *The Passing of Traditional Society* (Glencoe, Ill.: Free Press, 1957); Rostow, *The Stages of Economic Growth;* Seymour M. Lipset, *Political Man: The Social Bases of Politics* (New York: Anchor, 1963); David Apter, *The Politics of Modern-*

ization (Chicago: University of Chicago Press, 1965); Samuel Huntington, *Political Order in Changing Society* (New Haven, Conn.: Yale University Press, 1968). For a recent assessment of modernization theory, see Zehra F. Arat, "Democracy and Economic Development: Modernization Theory Revisited," *Comparative Politics* (October 1988):21–36; Alvin Y. So, *Social Change and Development: Modernization, Dependency, and World Systems Theories* (Newbury Park, Calif.: Sage Publications, 1990).

35. For an introduction to dependency and world systems theories, see Ronald H. Chilcote, *Theories of Development and Underdevelopment* (Boulder, Colo.: Westview Press, 1984).

36. Karl Marx, *Capital: A Critique of Political Economy*, ed. Friedrich Engels (New York: International Publishers, 1967; orig. pub. 1848).

37. World Bank, *World Development Report 1992*, 223.

38. UNDP, *Human Development Report 1992*, 101–103.

39. Mahesh Banskota, "Foreign Aid and the Poor," in Integrated Development Systems, ed., *Proceedings, Seminar on Foreign Aid and Development in Nepal* (Kathmandu, Nepal: Integrated Development Systems, 1983).

40. George Honadle and Jerry VanSant, *Implementation for Sustainability: Lessons from Integrated Rural Development* (West Hartford, Conn.: Kumarian Press, 1985), 103–110.

41. Jon R. Moris, *Managing Induced Rural Development* (Bloomington, Ind.: International Development Institute, 1981), 93; see also Paul Streeten, *First Things First: Meeting Basic Human Needs in Developing Countries* (New York: Oxford University Press, 1981).

42. See David Pearce, Edward Barbier, and Anil Markandya, *Sustainable Development: Economics and Environment in the Third World* (Aldershot: Edward Elger Publishing Limited, 1990).

43. See Robert Klitgaard, *Adjusting to Reality: Beyond "State Versus Market" in Economic Development* (San Francisco: ICS Press, 1991); Giovanni A. Cornia, Richard Jolly, and Frances Stewart, eds., *Adjustment with a Human Face: Protecting the Vulnerable and Promoting Growth* (New York: Oxford University Press for UNICEF, 1987).

CHAPTER THREE

1. Merilee S. Grindle, ed., *Politics and Policy Implementation in the Third World* (Princeton, N.J.: Princeton University Press, 1980); Susan George, *How the Other Half Dies: The Real Reasons for World Hunger* (Middlesex: Penguin Books, 1977).

2. See Derek E. Tribe, *Doing Well by Doing Good: Agricultural Research and the Greening of the World* (Leichhardt, Australia: Pluto Press, 1991); Wayne E. Swegle and Polly C. Ligon, eds., *Aid, Trade, and Farm Policies: A Sourcebook on Issues and Interrelationships* (Morrilton, Ark.: Winrock International Institute for Agricultural Development, 1989); and Robert Paarlberg, "Connections Between Agricultural Development in Poor Countries and the Prosperity of Agriculture in the U.S." (Paper presented at the American Agricultural Editors' Association Leadership Conference, Winrock International Institute for Agricultural Development, Morrilton, Arkansas, July 1990).

3. A target of 1.0 percent was first proposed by the World Council of Churches in 1958, and a revised target of 0.7 percent was accepted as an international goal in the 1960s. See Organization for Economic Cooperation and Development (OECD), *Twenty-Five Years of Development Cooperation: A Review* (Paris: OECD, 1985), 135–137.

4. See Judith Tendler, *Inside Foreign Aid* (Baltimore: Johns Hopkins University Press, 1975); Susan George, *How the Other Half Dies*; Frances M. Lappe and Joseph Collins, *Food First: Beyond the Myth of Scarcity* (New York: Ballantine Books, 1977); Stephen Hellinger, Douglas Hellinger, and Fred M. O'Regan, *Aid for Just Development* (Boulder, Colo.: Lynne Rienner Publishers, 1988); Graham Hancock, *Lords of Poverty: The Power, Prestige, and Corruption of the International Aid Business* (New York: Atlantic Monthly Press, 1989); Richard Holloway, *Doing Development: Governments, NGOs, and the Rural Poor in Asia* (New York: Earthscan, 1989); Jan K. Black, *Development in Theory and Practice: Bridging the Gap* (Boulder, Colo.: Westview Press, 1991).

5. OECD, *Twenty-Five Years of Development Cooperation*, 133, 148.

6. OECD, *Development Cooperation: Efforts and Policies of the Members of the Development Assistance Committee* (Paris: OECD, 1991), 148. Multilateral organizations are less tied to individual state agenda than are bilateral agencies, but bilateral national security concerns can influence these organizations. For example, until late 1991, the Asian Development Bank (ADB) could not implement technical assistance projects and loans for Viet Nam, Laos, or Cambodia because the United States vetoed such proposals when they were presented for ADB board approval. This situation changed after the 1991 Cambodian Peace Accord was signed and the United States announced its intention to normalize relations with Viet Nam.

7. OECD, *Development Cooperation: Efforts and Policies of the Members of the Development Assistance Committee* (Paris: OECD, 1992), A-23.

8. Ibid., A-10, A-11.

9. World Bank, *World Development Report 1992* (New York: Oxford University Press, 1992), 256–257.

10. The United States divides its development aid into three categories: economic support funds, development assistance, and food aid. Economic support funds (ESF) are typically used for budget support to politically friendly governments. Most ESF funds have gone to Israel and Egypt since the Camp David Accords were signed by Israel, Egypt, and the United States in 1978. See OECD, *Development Cooperation: Efforts and Policies of the Members of the Development Assistance Committee* (1990), 153.

11. Roger East, ed., *Keesing's Record of World Events* (Cambridge: Longman, 1990, 1991), 36 (1990):37764; 37 (1991):38194.

12. United Nations Development Programme (UNDP), *Human Development Report 1991* (New York: Oxford University Press, 1991), 127–128.

13. East, *Keesing's Record of World Events*, 37 (1991):37961, 38195.

14. OECD, *Development Cooperation: Efforts and Policies of the Members of the Development Assistance Committee* (1992), A-58, A-64.

15. Michael B. Wallace, "Forest Degradation in Nepal: Institutional Context and Policy Alternatives," *Research Report Paper Series*, no. 6 (Kathmandu, Nepal: HMG-

USAID-GTZ-IDRC-Ford-Winrock Project, *Strengthening Institutional Capacity in the Food and Agricultural Sector in Nepal*, 1988), 26.

16. Dr. John C. Cool, personal communication.

17. OECD, *Development Cooperation: Efforts and Policies of the Members of the Development Assistance Committee* (1991), 206.

18. Uma Lele and Ijaz Nabi, eds., *Transitions in Development: The Role of Aid and Commercial Flows* (San Francisco: International Center for Economic Growth, 1991), 470–472.

19. East, *Keesing's Record of World Events*, 37 (1991):38176.

20. Since World War II, scholars have refined realism into a rigorous theory that concentrates on the systemic aspects of the international system of states and state behavior. Although the specific attributes of this system remain topics of debate for scholars, this discourse can be generally termed *neorealism*. In this book we refer to this dominant paradigm as realism; the classic neorealist text is Kenneth N. Waltz's *Theory of International Politics* (Reading, Mass.: Addison-Wesley, 1979). See also Robert O. Keohane, ed., *Neorealism and Its Critics* (New York: Columbia University Press, 1986).

21. United Nations Development Programme (UNDP), *Human Development Report 1992* (New York: Oxford University Press, 1992), 161, 166–167, 197, 206. Complete information is presented for 25 industrial countries and 75 developing countries.

22. Ibid., 162–163.

23. For international political economy literature written from a realist or neorealist perspective, see Robert Gilpin, *The Political Economy of International Relations* (Princeton, N.J.: Princeton University Press, 1987); Stephen Krasner, *Structural Conflict: The Third World Against Global Liberalism* (Berkeley: University of California Press, 1985); Stephen Krasner, ed., *International Regimes* (Ithaca, N.Y.: Cornell University Press, 1983); Keohane, *Neorealism and Its Critics*. For a critique of this literature, see Craig N. Murphy and Roger Tooze, eds., *The New International Political Economy* (Boulder, Colo.: Lynne Rienner Publishers, 1991).

24. Idealism refers to the tradition of international relations theory that parallels the realist and neorealist traditions. Idealist theories were somewhat discounted after World War II as incapable of explaining the Cold War and the emergence of superpowers. Idealism focuses on more humanitarian aspects of political behavior among states. Scholars concerned with international ethnics, distributive justice, international cooperation, human rights, and global futures have contributed to idealist theory. For further reading, see Charles Beitz, *Political Theory and International Relations* (Princeton, N.J.: Princeton University Press, 1979); Stanley Hoffman, *Duties Beyond Borders: On the Limits and Possibilities of Ethical International Relations* (Syracuse, N.Y.: Syracuse University Press, 1981); Lynn Miller, *Global Order* (Philadelphia: Temple University Press, 1986); Edward Weisband, *Poverty Amidst Plenty* (Boulder, Colo.: Westview Press, 1989).

25. J. D. Singer, "The Levels of Analysis Problem in International Relations," in James Rosenau, ed., *International Politics and Foreign Policy: A Reader in Research and Theory* (New York: Free Press, 1969), 21.

26. See Hoffman, *Duties Beyond Borders*.

27. See Johan Galtung, *The True Worlds* (New York: The Free Press, 1980); Samuel S. Kim, *The Quest for a Just World Order* (Boulder, Colo.: Westview Press, 1984); Melvin Gurtor, *Global Politics in the Human Interest* (Boulder, Colo.: Lynne Rienner Publishers, 1988); Ernst-Otto Czempiel and James N. Rosenau, eds., *Global Changes and Theoretical Challenges* (Lexington, Mass.: Lexington Books, 1989).

28. See Norman Uphoff and Warren F. Ilchman, eds., *The Political Economy of Development* (Berkeley: University of California Press, 1972); Robert O. Keohane and Joseph S. Nye, *Power and Interdependence* (Boston: Little, Brown, 1977); Galtung, *The True Worlds*; Richard Ashley, "Three Modes of Economism," *International Studies Quarterly* 27, no. 4 (1983):463–496; Robert O. Keohane, *After Hegemony: Cooperation and Discord in World Political Economy* (Princeton, N.J.: Princeton University Press, 1984); Robert Cox, *Production, Power, and World Order* (New York: Columbia University Press, 1987); Charles Wilber, ed., *The Political Economy of Development and Underdevelopment*, 4th ed. (New York: Random House, 1988); Susan Strange, *States and Markets: An Introduction to International Political Economy* (New York: Basil Blackwell Inc., 1988); Weisband, *Poverty Amidst Plenty*; Lev S. Gonick and Edward Weisband, *Teaching World Politics: Contending Pedagogies for a New World Order* (Boulder, Colo.: Westview Press, 1992).

29. See Adrienne Harris and Ynestra King, eds., *Rocking the Ship of State: Toward a Feminist Peace Politics* (Boulder, Colo.: Westview Press, 1989); Dennis S. Pirages and Christine Sylvester, eds., *Transformations in the Global Political Economy* (New York: St. Martin's Press, 1990); Cynthia Enloe, *Bananas, Beaches, and Bases: Making Feminist Sense of International Politics* (Berkeley: University of California Press, 1990); V. Spike Peterson, ed., *Gendered States: Feminist (Re)visions of International Relations* (Boulder, Colo.: Lynne Rienner Publishers, 1992); Murphy and Tooze, *The New Political Economy*.

30. Neo-Marxism denotes the theories, based on the philosophy of Karl Marx, that have been devised since World War II to explain the causes of poverty, underdevelopment, exploitation, militarism, and the expansion of international capital. For further explanation, see Black, *Development in Theory and Practice*; Anthony Brewer, *Marxist Theories of Imperialism: A Critical Survey* (London: Routledge and Kegan Paul, 1980); V. Kubalkova and A. A. Cruickshank, *International Inequality: Competing Approaches* (New York: St. Martin's Press, 1981); Ronald H. Chilcote, *Theories of Development and Underdevelopment* (Boulder, Colo.: Westview Press, 1984).

31. Raul Prebisch, *The Economic Development of Latin America and Its Principal Problems* (New York: United Nations, 1950).

32. Theotonio Dos Santos, "The Structure of Dependence," *American Economic Review* 60, no. 2 (May 1970):231–236; Andre Gundar Frank, *Dependent Accumulation and Development* (New York: Monthly Review Press, 1973); Fernando Cardoso and Enzo Falletto, *Dependency and Underdevelopment in Latin America* (Berkeley: University of California Press, 1979).

33. Immanuel Wallerstein, *The Modern World System: Capitalist Agriculture and the Origins of the European World-Economy in the Sixteenth Century* (New York: Academic Press, 1974); Immanuel Wallerstein, *The Capitalist World Economy* (New York: Academic Press, 1979).

34. Brian H. Smith, *More Than Altruism: The Politics of Private Foreign Aid* (Princeton, N.J.: Princeton University Press, 1990).

35. Nonprofit organizations must be accountable to the public in most developed countries in order to secure tax-exempt status or other privileges granted by governments. Governments may curtail these privileges if organizations engage in political activity.

36. Smith, *More Than Altruism.*

37. Mark Ufkes, personal communication.

38. Smith, *More Than Altruism*, 65.

39. The term *mercenary* should not be taken as excessively negative. Mercenary means working for pay, which is what private-sector for-profit and nonprofit development practitioners do.

40. For a critical review of the history and motivations underlying the activities of the Asian Development Bank, a major donor in Asia, see James Clad, "Unhappy Returns: The Asian Development Bank Rumbles with Discontent," *Far Eastern Economic Review,* November 27, 1986, 60–69.

41. Tendler, *Inside Foreign Aid*, 102.

42. "Monday Developments," *INTERACTION,* October 10, 1990, 10.

43. Smith, *More Than Altruism*, 282.

CHAPTER FOUR

1. George Rosen, *Western Economists and Eastern Societies: Agents of Change in South Asia, 1950–70* (Delhi: Oxford University Press, 1985), 5.

2. Ibid., 5–12.

3. Ibid., 5.

4. Ibid., 4–6.

5. See Marc Lindenberg and Benjamin Crosby, *Managing Development: The Political Dimension* (West Hartford, Conn.: Kumarian Press, 1981).

6. Coralie Bryant and Louise White, *Managing Development in the Third World* (Boulder, Colo.: Westview Press, 1982), 52–53. See also Susan Rose-Ackerman, *Corruption: A Study in Political Economy* (New York: Academic Press, 1978).

7. Sally W. Yudelman, *Hopeful Openings: A Study of Five Women's Development Organizations in Latin America and the Caribbean* (West Hartford, Conn.: Kumarian Press, 1987).

8. David Ignatius, "A Vietnamese Village and Its 25-Year Return from the Ashes," *International Herald Tribune,* November 12, 1991, 2. See also Jonathan Schell, *The Village of Ben Suc* (New York: Knopf, 1967).

9. Kathryn S. March and Rachelle L. Taqqu, *Women's Informal Associations in Developing Countries: Catalysts for Change?* (Boulder, Colo.: Westview Press, 1986); Norman T. Uphoff and Milton J. Esman, *Local Organizations: Intermediaries in Rural Development* (Ithaca, N.Y.: Cornell University Press, 1984).

10. There are many new methodology handbooks on participatory research and implementation. See J. McCracken, J. Pretty, and G. Conway, *An Introduction to Rapid Rural Appraisal for Agricultural Development* (London: International Institute for Environment and Development, 1989); R. Chambers, A. Pacey, and L. A. Thrupp, eds., *Farmer First: Farmer Innovation and Agricultural Research* (London: In-

termediate Technology Publications, 1989); Krishna Kumar, "Conducting Group Interviews in Developing Countries," *A.I.D. Program Design and Evaluation Methodology Report No. 8* (Washington, D.C.: U.S. Agency for International Development, 1987); Clive Lightfoot, Shelly Feldman, and M. Zainul Abedin, *Households, Agroecosystems, and Rural Resources Management* (Joydepur, Bangladesh; and Manila: Bangladesh Agricultural Research Institute and the International Center for Living Aquatic Resources Management, 1991).

11. Irene Tinker, *Persistent Inequalities: Women and World Development* (New York: Oxford University Press, 1990).

12. Ibid.

13. Alice S. Carloni, "Women in FAO Projects: Cases from Asia, the Near East, and Africa," in Kathleen Staudt, ed., *Women, International Development, and Politics: The Bureaucratic Mire* (Philadelphia: Temple University Press, 1990), 227–246; Edwin G. Brush and Anu R. Rao, "Issues of Professional Women in Agricultural Research in Developing Countries," *Staff Notes* (The Hague: International Service for National Agricultural Research, June 1991); Rae Lesser Blumberg, "Making the Case for the Gender Variable: Women and the Wealth and Well-Being of Nations," *Technical Reports in Gender and Development* (Washington, D.C.: Office of·Women in Development, U.S. Agency for International Development, 1989); Janice Jiggins, "Gender-Related Impacts and the Work of the International Agricultural Research Centers," *CGIAR Study Paper No. 17* (Washington, D.C.: World Bank, 1986); Alice S. Carloni, "Women in Development: A.I.D.'s Experience, 1973–1985," vol. 1, Synthesis Paper, *A.I.D. Program Evaluation Report No. 18* (Washington, D.C.: U.S. Agency for International Development, 1987).

14. Kathleen Staudt, "Context and Politics in the Gendered Bureaucratic Mire," in Staudt, *Women, International Development, and Politics, 304–313*; Nancy McGlen and Meredith R. Sarkees, "Foreign Policy, Bureaucracies, and Women's Influence: Rules and Structure," Paper presented at the 1989 Annual Meeting of the American Political Science Association, Atlanta, August 31–September 3, 1989.

15. Cynthia Enloe, *Beaches, Bananas, and Bases: Making Feminist Sense of International Politics* (Berkeley: University of California Press, 1990), 3.

16. Katarina Tomasevski, *Development Aid and Human Rights: A Study for the Danish Center of Human Rights* (New York: St. Martin's Press, 1989); Carloni, "Women in FAO Projects."

17. Dr. John De Boer, personal communication.

18. Ernst Haas, *When Knowledge Is Power: Three Models of Change in International Organizations* (Berkeley: University of California Press, 1990), 40.

19. Ibid., 42.

20. See Cheryl Payer, *The Debt Trap: The International Monetary Fund and the Third World* (Hammondsworth: Penguin Books, 1974); Cheryl Payer, *The World Bank: A Critical Analysis* (New York: Monthly Review Press, 1982); Stanley Please, *The Hobbled Giant: Essays on the World Bank* (Boulder, Colo.: Westview Press, 1982).

21. The Hash House Harriers is open to anyone who is interested, but expatriates tend to be the most active participants in this informal club.

CHAPTER FIVE

1. See Raymond Hopkins, "Aid for Development: What Motivates the Donors," in Edward Clay and John Shaw, eds., *Poverty, Development, and Food* (London: Macmillan Press, 1987), 154.

2. See the discussion in Chapter 3 on the international development assistance regime. See also ibid., 153–160.

3. See G. O. Nelson, C. P. Timmer, M. Guerreiro, G. Edward Schuh, and P. Alailima, *Food Aid and Development* (New York: Agricultural Development Council, 1981); Cheryl Christensen, Edward B. Hogan, Bede N. Okigbo, G. Edward Schuh, Edward J. Clay, and John W. Thomas, *The Developmental Effectiveness of Food Aid in Africa* (New York: Agricultural Development Council, 1982); Frances Stewart, "Adjustment with a Human Face: The Role of Food Aid," *Food Policy* 13 (1988):18–26; Deborah Clubb and Polly Ligon, eds., *Food, Hunger, and Agricultural Issues* (Morrilton, Ark.: Winrock International, 1989); Graham Hancock, *Lords of Poverty: The Power, Prestige, and Corruption of the International Aid Business* (New York: Atlantic Monthly Press, 1989).

4. OECD, *Development Cooperation: Efforts and Policies of the Development Assistance Committee* (Paris: OECD, 1991), 172.

5. Hopkins, "Aid for Development," 157.

6. Ibid., 167.

7. David C. Korten, *Getting to the 21st Century: Voluntary Action and the Global Agenda* (West Hartford, Conn.: Kumarian Press, 1990), iv.

8. See Teresa Hayter, *Aid as Imperialism* (Baltimore: Penguin, 1971); Judith Tendler, *Inside Foreign Aid* (Baltimore: Johns Hopkins University Press, 1975); Teresa Hayter and Catherine Watson, *Aid: Rhetoric and Reality* (London: Pluto Press, 1985); Hopkins, "Aid for Development"; Douglas Dowd, *The Waste of Nations: Dysfunction in the World Economy* (Boulder, Colo.: Westview Press, 1989).

9. See Andre Gunder Frank, "The Development of Underdevelopment," *Monthly Review* 18, no. 4 (1966); Fernando H. Cardoso and Enzo Falletto, *Dependency and Development in Latin America* (Berkeley: University of California Press, 1979); Denis Goulet, *The Cruel Choice: A New Concept in the Theory of Development* (New York: Atheneum, 1971); Godfrey Gunatilleke, Neelen Tirchelvam, and Radhika Coomaraswamy, eds., *Ethical Dilemmas of Development in Asia* (Lexington, Mass.: Lexington Books, 1983); P. T. Bauer, *Equality, the Third World, and Economic Delusion* (London: Weidenfeld, 1981); S. C. Dube, *Modernization and Development: The Search for Alternative Paradigms* (London: Zed Books Ltd., 1988); Charles K. Wilber, ed., *The Political Economy of Development and Underdevelopment*, 4th ed. (New York: Random House, 1988); Edward Weisband, *Poverty Amidst Plenty: World Political Economy and Distributive Justice* (Boulder, Colo.: Westview Press, 1989); David A. Crocker, "Toward Development Ethics," *World Development* 19, no. 5 (1991):457–483.

10. See Giovanni A. Cornia, Richard Jolly, and Frances Stewart, eds., *Adjustment with a Human Face: Protecting the Vulnerable and Promoting Growth* (New York: Oxford University Press for UNICEF, 1987).

11. See Michael Lipton, *Why Poor People Stay Poor: Urban Bias in World Development* (Cambridge, Mass.: Harvard University Press, 1976); Michael Lipton with

Richard Longhurst, *New Seeds for Poor People* (Baltimore: Johns Hopkins University Press, 1989).

12. P. Pingali, P. F. Moya, and L. E. Velasco, "The Post-Green Revolution Blues in Asian Rice Production," *Social Science Division Papers,* no. 90-01, International Rice Research Institute, 1991.

13. See Hancock, *Lords of Poverty.*

14. See United Nations Development Programme (UNDP), *Human Development Report 1992* (New York: Oxford University Press, 1992).

15. See Amartya Sen, *Resources, Values, and Development* (Cambridge, Mass.: Harvard University Press, 1984).

16. Crocker, "Toward Development Ethics," 458–459.

17. Weisband, *Poverty Amidst Plenty,* 10.

18. UNDP, *Human Development Report 1992,* 162–163.

19. See the Notes to Chapter Two for a list of the 24 countries with annual average per capita GNPs of less than $300.

20. UNDP, *Human Development Report 1992,* 152–153.

21. Jan K. Black, *Development in Theory and Practice: Bridging the Gap* (Boulder, Colo.: Westview Press, 1991), 139.

22. See ibid.

23. Pramod Parajuli, "Power and Knowledge in Development Discourse: New Social Movements and the State in India," *International Conflict Research* 127 (February 1991):173–190.

24. Elliot R. Morss and Virginia A. Morss, *U.S. Foreign Aid: An Assessment of New and Traditional Development Strategies* (Boulder, Colo.: Westview Press, 1982); Elliot R. Morss and Virginia A. Morss, *The Future of Development Assistance* (Boulder, Colo.: Westview Press, 1986); Stephen Hellinger, Douglas Hellinger, and Fred M. O'Regan, *Aid for Just Development* (Boulder, Colo.: Lynne Rienner Publishers, 1988); Black, *Development in Theory and Practice.*

25. See Korten, *Getting to the 21st Century.*

26. Jimmy Carter, "The Third World Is Not a Hopeless Place," *New Age Journal* (March/April 1990):53–54, 132–134.

27. See Harka Gurung, "Economic Implications of Foreign Aid," in Integrated Development Systems, ed., *Proceedings, Seminar on Foreign Aid and Development in Nepal* (Kathmandu, Nepal: Integrated Development Systems, 1983).

28. Uma Lele and Ijaz Nabi, *Transitions in Development: The Role of Aid and Commercial Flows* (San Francisco: International Center for Economic Growth, 1991).

29. Ibid., 470–472.

30. Ibid., 472–474.

31. Data collection is improving in developing countries; this supports the efforts of international organizations that analyze the data and publish cross-country comparisons, such as the World Bank (*World Development Report*) and the United Nations Development Programme (*Human Development Report*).

32. Vernon W. Ruttan, "Sustainable Growth in Agricultural Production: Poetry, Policy, and Science," *Department of Agricultural and Applied Economics Staff Paper P91-47* (Minneapolis: Department of Agricultural and Applied Economics, University of Minnesota, 1991), 3–5.

33. Sandra Batie, "Sustainable Development: Challenges to the Profession of Agricultural Economics," *American Journal of Agricultural Economics* 71, no. 5 (December 1989):1085–1101.

34. See Sen, *Resources, Values, and Development*.

35. See OECD, *Twenty-Five Years of Development Cooperation: A Review* (Paris: OECD, 1985).

36. Robert Klitgaard, *Adjusting to Reality: Beyond "State Versus Market" in Economic Development* (San Francisco: ICS Press, 1991).

37. We are indebted to Dr. John C. Cool for this insight.

□ □ □

Suggested Readings

Bartelmus, Peter. *Environment and Development*. Boston: Allen and Unwin, 1986.

Berger, Peter L., and Michael Novak. *Speaking to the Third World: Essays on Democracy and Development*. Washington, D.C.: American Enterprise Institute, 1985.

Brookfield, Harold. *Interdependent Development*. Pittsburgh: University of Pittsburgh Press, 1975.

Casson, Robert. *Does Aid Work?* Oxford: Clarendon Press, 1986.

Cernea, Michael M. *Putting People First: Sociological Variables in Rural Development*. New York: Oxford University Press, 1985.

Chilcote, Ronald H. *Theories of Development and Underdevelopment*. Boulder, Colo.: Westview Press, 1984.

Dwyer, Daisy, and Judith Bruce, eds. *A House Divided: Women and Income in the Third World*. Stanford: Stanford University Press, 1988.

Feinberg, Richard. *Between Two Worlds: The World Bank's Next Decade*. New Brunswick, N.J.: Transaction Books, 1986.

Feldstein, Hilary S., and Susan V. Poats. *Working Together: Gender Issues in Agriculture*, vol. 1. Westport, Conn.: Kumarian Press, 1989.

Gallin, Rita S., and Anne Ferguson. *The Women in Development Annual*, vol. 2. Boulder, Colo.: Westview Press, 1991.

Gallin, Rita S., Marilyn Aronoff, and Anne Ferguson. *The Women in Development Annual*, vol. 1. Boulder, Colo.: Westview Press, 1989.

George, Susan. *Ill Faces the Land: Essays on Food, Hunger, and Power*. Washington, D.C.: Institute for Policy Studies, 1986.

Gillis, Malcolm, Dwight H. Perkins, Michael Roemer, and Donald R. Snodgrass. *Economics of Development*. New York: W. W. Norton, 1983.

Gorman, R. F. *PVOs as Agents of Development*. Boulder, Colo.: Westview Press, 1985.

Hirschman, Albert O. *The Strategy of Economic Development*. Boulder, Colo.: Westview Press, 1988.

Hunter, Guy. *Agricultural Development and the Rural Poor*. London: Overseas Development Institute, 1978.

Johnson, B.L.C. *Development in South Asia*. New York: Penguin Books, 1983.

Korten, David C., and Rudi Klass, eds. *People-Centered Development: Contributions Toward Theory and Planning Frameworks*. West Hartford, Conn.: Kumarian Press, 1984.

Krueger, Anne, and Vernon Ruttan. *The Development Impact of Economic Assistance to LDCs*, vols. 1 and 2. Washington, D.C.: U.S. Agency for International Development, 1983.

Loehr, William, and John P. Powelson. *Economic Development, Poverty, and Income Distribution*. Boulder, Colo.: Westview Press, 1977.

McNamara, Robert. "Time Bomb or Myth: The Population Problem." *Foreign Affairs* 62, nos. 4–5 (Summer 1984):1107–1131.

Meier, Gerald M. *Emerging from Poverty: The Economics That Really Matter*. Oxford: Oxford University Press, 1984.

————. *Politics and Policy Making in Developing Countries: Perspectives on the New Political Economy*. San Francisco: ICS Press, 1991.

Nelson, G. O., C. P. Timmer, M. Guerreiro, G. Edward Schuh, and P. Alailima. *Food Aid and Development*. New York: Agricultural Development Council, 1981.

Nelson, Joan. *Fragile Coalitions: The Politics of Economic Adjustment*. New Brunswick, N.J.: Transaction Books, 1989.

Overholt, Catherine, Mary B. Anderson, Kathleen Cloud, and James E. Austin. *Gender Roles in Development Projects*. West Hartford, Conn.: Kumarian Press, 1985.

Paarlberg, Don. *Farmers of Five Continents*. Lincoln: University of Nebraska Press, 1984.

Paul, Samuel. *Managing Development Programs: The Lessons of Success*. Boulder, Colo.: Westview Press, 1982.

Post, Ken, and Phil Wright. *Socialism and Underdevelopment*. London: Routledge, 1989.

Riddell, Roger. *Foreign Aid Reconsidered*. Baltimore: Johns Hopkins University Press, 1987.

Rostow, Walter W. *Rich Countries and Poor Countries: Reflections on the Past, Lessons for the Future*. Boulder, Colo.: Westview Press, 1987.

Russell, Clifford S., and Norman K. Nicholson. *Public Choice and Rural Development*. Washington, D.C.: Resources for the Future, 1981.

Steidlmeier, Paul. "Models of Development and Social Change." In Edward Weisband, ed., *Poverty Amidst Plenty: World Political Economy and Distributive Justice*. Boulder, Colo.: Westview Press, 1989, 89–109.

Stevens, Robert D., and Cathy L. Jabara. *Agricultural Development Principles: Economic Theory and Empirical Evidence*. Baltimore: Johns Hopkins University Press, 1988.

Taylor, Lance. *Varieties of Stabilization Experiences: Toward Macroeconomics in the Third World*. New York: Oxford University Press, 1988.

Timmer, C. Peter, ed. *Agriculture and the State: Growth, Employment, and Poverty in Developing Countries*. Ithaca, N.Y.: Cornell University Press, 1991.

United Nations Economic, Social and Cultural Organization (UNESCO). *Goals of Development*. Paris: UNESCO, 1988.

Yudelman, Montague. "The World Bank and Agricultural Development: An Insider's View." *World Resources Institute Paper No. 1*. Washington, D.C.: World Resources Institute, 1985.

□ □ □

Recommended Resources

Brenda Markovitz

This listing includes the most recent and useful films and educational television materials available. Although not exhaustive, it contains the geographical and topical diversity to reinforce the concepts and themes presented in this text.

Africa in Focus. 7 programs, each 20 minutes, 1990.
> These programs give an overview of several African nations that examines geography, sociology, culture, economy, and future outlook. Journal Films.

Africa Tomorrow. 29 minutes, 1987.
> Using clips from the Live Aid Concert, this film displays the devastating effects of the African drought. New Dimensions Films.

An African Recovery. 28 minutes, 1988.
> This film examines the causes of devastating droughts in the North River Valley in Africa and shows recovery projects that are now in effect to prevent them from recurring. Icarus Films.

The Africans. 9-part series, each part 60 minutes, 1986.
> 1. Nature of a Continent; 2. Legacy of Lifestyles; 3. New Gods; 4. Tools of Exploitation; 5. New Conflicts; 6. In Search of Stability; 7. Garden of Eden in Decay; 8. Clash of Cultures; 9. Global Africa. Each of these films examines a different aspect of African development. WETA/BBC.

Amazon: Paradise Lost? 60 minutes, 1992.
> This film offers a penetrating study of the ongoing destruction of the rainforests and the ensuing global consequences. Christian Science Monitor Video.

Assignment: Africa. 60 minutes, 1993.
> This country profile focuses on women's rights, democracy in Zambia, the AIDS epidemic in Tanzania, the collapse of the Nigerian oil industry, and several other informative and compelling points of focus on Africa today. Christian Science Monitor Video.

Assignment: China. 60 minutes, 1993.

This profile of China includes a view of sources of local power, a study of family planning in China, and a look at one of the five economic zones set up as part of China's economic reform. Christian Science Monitor Video.

Assignment: India. 60 minutes, 1993.

This country profile includes a look at Gandhi's legacy in a country torn apart by internal violence, a view of women today as they seek greater independence, and an examination of the issue of child labor. Christian Science Monitor Video.

Assignment: Southeast Asia. 60 minutes, 1993.

This profile examines the state of the region today as it deals with some of the painful aftereffects of war and includes a look at the resurgence of the pineapple industry. Christian Science Monitor Video.

The Avoidable Famine. 20 minutes, 1988.

This film examines Sudanese agriculture and the ways new methods of arming contribute to famine. Journal Films.

Bombay: Our City. 57 minutes, 1985.

This program looks at the daily lives of slum dwellers in Bombay, who make up half of the city's population and most of its labor force. Florida Folklife Programs.

Bread, Butter, and Politics. 60 minutes, 1984.

This PBS Frontline series focuses on hunger in America, examining the case of urban poverty in Chicago in particular. WGBH/PBS Video.

The Business of Hunger. 25 minutes, 1984.

The film presents one major cause of hunger in the world today—agribusiness practices that export food from hungry nations. Maryknoll Media Relations.

Central America: Close-Up. 60 minutes, 1988.

This film focuses on how the youth of Honduras and Nicaragua deal with war and issues of economic development. Maryknoll World Video.

Central America: On the Horns of a Dilemma. 29 minutes, 1988.

The problems associated with deforestation in Central America are addressed in this video. University of Kentucky.

Children in Debt. 29 minutes, 1987.

Latin America's debt crisis and its effect on children are examined. Cinema Guild.

Chile: The Impact of Third World Debt. Life-Choice series. 29 minutes, 1990.

The film assesses the impact of international debt on the political and economic development of Chile. Golden Dome Productions.

Development Without Tears. 27 minutes, 1978.

This film argues that real economic development in poor countries involves the creation of wealth and its even distribution throughout society. National Film Board of Canada.

The Devil Gave Us Oil. 60 minutes, 1987.

This program explores the oil industry in Mexico and follows the life of a typical farmer and his family in their struggle to survive in the shadow of an oil refinery and its polluted environment. PBS Video.

Earth: The Changing Environment. 30 minutes, 1987.

This program probes the ecological consequences of improper economic development. PBS Video.

Economic Systems. Sociological Imagination series. 30 minutes, 1991.

This program explores the relationships among economy, culture, and family. Dallas Telecourses.

Education. Sociological Imagination series. 30 minutes, 1991.

This program explores the relationships among education, society, and political and economic institutions. Dallas Telecourses.

From Sunup. 28 minutes, 1987.

Maryknoll World Video documents the daily lives of Tanzanian women as they seek to take their place in society, as influenced by their levels of education and the impact of Western civilization. Maryknoll World Video.

Garden of Eden in Decay? African series #7. 60 minutes, 1986.

This segment from the series *The Africans* identifies the problems of a continent that consumes what it does not produce and produces what it does not consume. This film shows Africa's struggle between economic dependency and decay. Annenberg/CPB project.

Global Assembly Line, Parts 1 & 2. 60 minutes, 1986.

This film follows the lives of working people in free trade zones of developing countries, Mexico and the Philippines in particular, focusing on the working conditions of these people. NewDay.

The Global Gamble. 60 minutes, 1987.
This program considers the world's oil market with a look at the most spectacular losing gamble in recent years, British Petroleum's loss of millions of dollars in unsuccessful drilling in the waters off mainland China. PBS Video.

Global Links. 6-part series. 1987.
Filmed in Asia, Africa, and Latin America, *Global Links* examines the quest for social and economic progress in those nations that account for more than 70 percent of the world's population. WETA/World Bank/PBS Video.

A Habitat Turned Hothouse. 22 minutes, 1989.
In this program, the greenhouse effect and the resulting damage to the environment are examined. PBS Video.

In the Name of Progress. Race to Save the Planet series. 60 minutes, 1990.
Economic development often results in environmental disasters. Can economic development and environmental protection coexist? WGBH/PBS Video.

Inside the Cartel. 60 minutes, 1990.
PBS's "Frontline" examines the power of Colombia's drug lords and the impact of their vast wealth on this South American nation. PBS Video.

It Needs Political Decisions. Race to Save the Planet series. 60 minutes, 1990.
This film focuses on three countries at different phases of economic development—Zimbabwe, Thailand, and Sweden—offering three different strategies for assuring a safe environmental future. WGBH/PBS Video.

Keeping People Alive: Malnutrition, the Hidden Killer. Five Minutes to Midnight series. 25 minutes, 1976.
The day-in, day-out erosion of physical and mental health caused by malnutrition is examined in this video. World Focus Ltd.

Life and Death in Rio. 25 minutes, 1987.
This film examines the plight of Rio's 9 million citizens and the substandard housing, poor nutrition, underemployment, and nonexistent sanitation they live with each day. BBC-TV.

Living Maya. 4 episodes. 60 minutes, 1982.
This film depicts the daily life of a community trying to maintain a balance between tradition and modernity. Kuxtal Productions.

Man Made Famine. 60 minutes, 1987.
Three African women tell of their daily struggle to feed their families. Their efforts are often stifled by a male-dominated culture that views farming as demeaning work. Filmakers Library, Inc.

More for Less. Race to Save the Planet series. 60 minutes, 1990.
WGBH and PBS Video explore ways to harness energy more efficiently while distributing economic benefits to society. WGBH/PBS Video.

Nicaragua: Development Under Fire. 26 minutes, 1986.
This program examines the economic situation in Nicaragua, the effects of the Contra War, and the political intricacies of international aid. Icarus Films.

The Oil Age. 26 minutes, 1984.
This film documents the history of oil exploration and its limited use for light and heat through the centuries. VISNEWS.

Oil and Water. 60 minutes, 1987.
This program highlights the exploitation of North Sea oil. PBS Video.

One World. 52 minutes, 1988.
Three kids go to India, Central America, and Africa to witness some of the problems the world is facing today. Journal Films, Inc.

The Other Side of the Border. 60 minutes, 1987.
This program examines the economic and political problems caused by illegal immigration and the exploitation of Mexican workers by U.S. employers. PBS Video.

Peace Dividend with Seymour Melman. 30 minutes, 1990.
Dr. Melman discusses ways to convert military spending to peacetime uses. PBS Video.

Philippine Diary. 28 minutes, 1988.
Four short features depict the horrible living conditions that led to the rise of the Aquino government.

The Price of Hunger. 21 minutes, 1987.
The causes of, and solutions to, world hunger are examined. Barr Films.

The Price of Progress. 54 minutes, 1990.
Resettlement programs in India, Brazil, and other countries—all sponsored by the World Bank—are examined. Bullfrog Films, Inc.

Power in the Pacific. 60 minutes, 1990.
This film looks at Japan's continually growing economic strength and possible sources of tension with the United States. PBS Video.

Religions of the Book: The Poor. Life-Choice series. 29 minutes, 1991.
This film discusses how the world's three great religions view poverty. Golden Dome Productions.

Retooling the Arms Industry. 29 minutes, 1990.
This film looks at how business and industry can cope with the economic changes brought about by the military builddown. Center for Defense Information/Video Project.

The Rise of OPEC. 60 minutes, 1987.
This program charts the rise of OPEC, which has become central in world oil supply and demand. PBS Video.

Santa Marta: Two Weeks in the Slums. 54 minutes, 1988.
This video shows the side of Rio de Janeiro tourists do not see: the mountaintop slum of Santa Marta. Cinema Guild.

Saudi Arabia: A Race with Time. 59 minutes, 1982.
This film examines the effects of a multibillion dollar surplus on Saudi Arabian society as it undergoes a period of accelerated modernization. Pacific Prod.

Sharing the Land. 20 minutes, 1988.
The reasons Brazil's economic boom of the 1970s did not trickle down to the poor are examined. Journal Films.

Sisters Under Siege. 60 minutes, 1987.
This program explores the roots of the Iran-Iraq War and the exploitation of oil in the Middle East. PBS Video.

Slums in the Third World. 17 minutes, 1984.
This film follows the daily life of the Sulayta family, which lives in a typical slum of a large Third World city. Phoenix/BFA Films.

Social Class. Sociological Imagination series. 30 minutes, 1991.
This film explores social class in the United States by focusing on two teenage girls from different social classes. Dallas Telecourses.

South America Today Series. 3 programs, each 20 minutes, 1990.
Colorful computer graphics are used to illustrate the supply and location of natural resources in South America's major nations. Journal Films, Inc.

Starving for Sugar. 58 minutes, 1988.
This film documents the stories of individual workers who have been hurt by the world decline in the sugar industry. Maryknoll World Productions.

The Storm of Acid Snow. 22 minutes, 1989.
Leading environmentalists and Arctic experts discuss the effects of airborne pol-
lutants and suggest that the pollution in the Arctic may cause the polar ice cap to
melt, which would elevate sea levels, causing flooding worldwide. PBS Video.

The Time Bomb. 27 minutes, 1989.
The financial crisis in Latin America is examined. United Nations/Cinema
Guild.

Tools of Exploitation. African series #4. 60 minutes, 1986.
This film contrasts the impact of the West on Africa and the impact of Africa on
the development of the West and focuses on the exploitation of colonialism.
Annenberg/CPG project.

Traditions and the 20th Century. 30 minutes, 1987.
This program offers a broad overview of six countries from West Africa to India
and examines the prospect for the survival of traditional cultures in the face of
modernization and development. PBS Video.

Water of Ayole. 38 minutes, 1989.
This film shows how a poor village in the West African nation of Togo is making
its new water system work. UNDP.

Water Supply and Sanitation in Development. 3 programs, each 30 minutes, 1985.
These videos focus on effective water management and sewage treatment sys-
tems in developing nations, including Nepal, Malawi, and Burma. World Bank/
United Nations.

Weaving the Future: Women of Guatemala. 28 minutes, 1988.
This fast-paced documentary explores the pivotal role women are playing in
building a just society in the midst of terrorism, political strife, and poverty.
Women Make Movies.

Women in the Third World. 30 minutes, 1987.
This program examines the living conditions of women throughout the developing world. World Bank/PBS Video.

□ □ □

Glossary

Adult literacy rate is the percentage of people age 15 and over who can, with understanding, both read and write a short, simple statement on everyday life.

Basic needs are those essential for a healthy and happy life: food, clean water, primary education, clothing, shelter, and access to health care.

Bilateral activities involve two states.

Bottom up refers to participatory development that involves beneficiaries in the design and implementation of development activities.

Capitalism is the system of production and consumption based on competitive private markets for goods and services, with little interference or guidance from the state.

Comparative advantage is a country's ability to produce a commodity at less cost (in terms of other commodities that might be produced instead) than other countries can produce it.

Cultural imperialism occurs when one society imposes its values on another.

Dependency theory explains the underdevelopment and poverty of poorer countries in terms of their dependence on richer countries for various historical reasons within the context of the expansion of capitalism.

Developing countries have low economic, health, and education levels. The World Bank divides 125 countries into 43 low-income economies, 58 middle-income economies, and 24 high-income economies; the UNDP divides 160 countries into 127 developing countries and 33 industrial countries.

Development aid projects are donor-funded activities designed to improve the lives of poor people in recipient countries.

Development assistance refers to resources provided by rich countries to help poor countries improve their living standards.

Dualism is the coexistence and persistence of increasing divergencies between rich and poor people.

Economic development theory attempts to explain how countries advance from poor to rich.

Expatriates are people who work in foreign countries.

Foreign aid refers to financial or in-kind assistance provided by one country to another.

Gender analysis is a methodology that helps identify access to, and control over, productive resources, income sources, expenditures, and division of labor between men and women.

161

Gender sensitivity is an approach that considers the presence of social, cultural, economic, and political inequalities or inequities that may exist between men and women.

Globalism is a perspective that views all states and nonstate actors as part of an overarching system of political, economic, and social interactions.

Grants are funds provided by donors without a commitment from the recipient to repay.

Green Revolution denotes the modern technology for producing rice, maize, and wheat by using high-yielding varieties of seed developed at international research centers. These seeds produce the best yields when they are used in combination with chemical fertilizer, irrigation, and pest control.

Gross domestic product (GDP) is the total final output of goods and services produced by a country's economy, regardless of allocation between domestic and foreign claims.

Gross national product (GNP) is the total domestic and foreign output claimed by the residents of a country; it excludes intermediate goods (which are used to produce other goods). GNP is GDP plus incomes accruing to residents from foreign sources minus domestic incomes accruing to persons abroad.

High-yielding varieties (HYV) of seed are hybrid seeds of rice, maize, and wheat, usually developed at international research centers, that—when used in combination with chemical fertilizer, irrigation, and pest control—produce higher yields than traditional varieties.

Human Development Index (HDI) is a measure of development that includes income (purchasing power parity), health (life expectancy), and education (literacy and years of schooling); the HDI is calculated by specifying minimum and desirable values for each indicator, indexing these end points, and averaging the three scales.

Human resource development involves productive investment in people (formal and informal education, short-term training) that enhances their skills and abilities.

Humanitarian aid is aid given primarily to benefit the recipient.

Idealism is a theoretical tradition in international relations which focuses on international cooperation and international law.

Industrial countries have high economic, health, and education levels (see "Developing countries").

Integrated rural development projects combine work in several sectors—typically agriculture, health, education, and income generation—in recognition of the interrelated nature of these aspects of development.

International political economy is the study of political and economic interactions among sovereign states.

International relations theory attempts to analyze power relations among state and nonstate actors in the international system.

Life expectancy is the average length of life in a particular country. It is the number of years a newborn infant could expect to live if prevailing patterns of mortality at the time of its birth were to stay the same throughout its life.

Loans are funds provided by donors that involve a commitment from the recipient to repay.

Marxism is the economic, political, and social theory based on the work of Karl Marx and Friedrich Engels.

Modernization is a theory of progress that relies on an evolutionary perspective: Social change is unidirectional, society moves from primitive to advanced, progress is good, and change is incremental.

Multilateral activities involve many states.

Multilateral development organizations have many states as members; prominent among these organizations are the United Nations and the World Bank.

Nationals are the citizens of a country.

Neo-Marxism refers to the theories, based on the philosophy of Karl Marx, that explain the causes of poverty, underdevelopment, exploitation, militarism, and the expansion of international capital since World War II.

Neorealism refers to refinements in the realist paradigm of international relations theory that also consider economic motivations of sovereign states.

Nongovernmental organizations (NGOs) are typically nonprofit, nonofficial organizations that are actively involved in the process of socioeconomic development. These organizations can be local, national, or international in scope, and they rely on donations or grants for their operations.

Normative theory attempts to prescribe how countries can advance from being poor to being rich.

Official Development Assistance (ODA) comprises flows from donor governments to recipient governments or multilateral organizations. Private agencies, such as philanthropic foundations, also provide funds for development purposes, usually to private recipient organizations or individuals.

Pluralism is a perspective that focuses on the diversity of state and nonstate actors within the world political system.

Politically motivated aid is aid given primarily to benefit the donor.

Private voluntary organizations (PVOs) are organizations supported primarily by private donations and for which service, not profit, is the primary motivation. This designation is used primarily in the United States; in other countries, similar organizations are called nongovernmental organizations (NGOs).

Purchasing power parity (PPP) is an international measure of income that is based on its ability to purchase goods and services rather than on official exchange rates.

Real GDP is an internationally comparable measure of income developed by the United Nations International Comparison Project. Real GDP uses purchasing power parities instead of official exchange rates to convert national currency figures to U.S. dollars; it thus provides a measure of the domestic purchasing power of these currencies.

Realism is a theory that explains sovereign state behavior; it focuses on security and accumulation of power within the context of a hostile international environment.

Regime refers to a set of norms or rules of behavior, based on formal or informal agreements, that provide a basis for institutions, conventions, and groups to address international conduct on particular issues.

Sectoral development projects focus on specific aspects of agriculture, industry, or services; they are often technology-oriented projects.

Socialism is an economic system in which all resources are state owned and their allocation and utilization are determined by central planning authorities rather than by prices based on market demand and supply.

Socioeconomic development is a complex process of improving people's lives. At a minimum, it involves advances in income, health, and education. However, development is more than the sum of these parts: Interactions among achievements and equitable distribution are also important, and people's participation in achieving higher living standards is often critical to sustaining development over time.

Sovereignty is the authority of the state, based on control of the legitimate use of force, recognized leadership with rules for succession, and recognition by other states and nonstate actors as the legitimate voice of the people.

Structural adjustment refers to policy and program recommendations developed by the World Bank and the International Monetary Fund to address the financial and economic development problems of developing countries.

Sustainable development recognizes that donor funding is limited and that the environmental costs of development must not be overlooked. This perspective attempts to ensure that local capability (both human skills and natural resources) can continue development activities after donor funding ceases.

Third World countries are poor, developing countries. This term is used in contrast to the First World (Western capitalist countries) and Second World (centrally planned economies of the former USSR and Eastern Europe).

Trickle down is the perspective in which development is considered to be an economic phenomenon in which gains from the growth of GNP (which may accrue initially to rich people) subsequently benefit poor people.

World political economy is a perspective that considers both political and economic interactions of state and nonstate actors.

World systems theory examines the political, social, and economic interactions of three sets of state and nonstate actors—core, semiperiphery, and periphery—within the context of a world capitalist market.

Years of schooling is the average duration of school attendance for persons age 25 and older.

Chronology

1944   Forty-four countries convene the United Nations (UN) Monetary and Financial Conference at Bretton Woods, New Hampshire. At the conference the International Bank for Reconstruction and Development (IBRD, or World Bank) and the International Monetary Fund (IMF) are established. Both organizations begin operations in 1946.

1945   The UN Charter is signed in San Francisco, establishing the United Nations and providing a framework for multilateral cooperation for the "promotion of economic and social advancement of all peoples."

1945   The Food and Agriculture Organization (FAO) of the United Nations is established.

1945   The United Kingdom strengthens its development assistance to colonies through the Colonial Development and Welfare Act.

1946   The UN General Assembly creates the UN International Children's Emergency Fund (UNICEF) and the UN Educational, Scientific and Cultural Organization (UNESCO).

1946   France establishes the *Fonds d'Investissement economique et social des territoires foutre-mer* (Fund for Social and Economic Investment of Overseas Territories) to provide assistance to its colonies.

1946   The UN Economic and Social Council (ECOSOC) Commission on Human Rights, Commission for Social Development, and Population Commission are established.

1947   The United States launches the Marshall Plan to assist European countries with cooperative reconciliation and reconstruction.

1947   The UN Economic Commission for Europe and the Economic and Social Commission for Asia and the Pacific are established.

1948   European recipients of Marshall Plan aid establish the Organization for European Economic Cooperation (OEEC).

1948   The World Health Organization (WHO) is established as a UN specialized agency.

1948   The United Kingdom establishes the Colonial Development Corporation, the British agency for providing development for its colonies.

1949   The United Nations establishes the Extended Programme of Technical Assistance.

1949   The OEEC establishes the Overseas Development Committee to survey the social and economic development of overseas territories of its members.

1949   The Council for Mutual Economic Assistance is established by the USSR.
1950   The U.S. Congress adopts President Harry Truman's Point Four Program of technical development assistance.
1950   The Colombo Plan for Cooperative Economic and Social Development in Asia and the Pacific is established by seven Commonwealth countries to promote interest in and support for the economic and social development of Asian and Pacific countries, review socioeconomic progress in the region, and facilitate development assistance to and within the region.
1952   U.S. development aid is disbursed through the Mutual Security Act, with major aid programs for Korea and Taiwan (Formosa).
1952   The U.S. Congress passes P.L. 480, providing a legal basis for food aid.
1955   Soviet development assistance begins with a Soviet-Indian agreement on construction of the Bhilai iron and steel works.
1956   The International Finance Corporation is established as an affiliate of the World Bank.
1957   The European Economic Community is established, as is the European Development Fund for Overseas Countries and Territories.
1958   The World Council of Churches calls for assistance to developing countries to be at least 1 percent of the incomes of rich countries.
1959   The United Nations creates a special fund to expand technical assistance and development activities.
1959   The Inter-American Development Bank is established.
1960   The World Bank establishes the International Development Association.
1960   Canada creates an External Aid Office for official development assistance.
1960   The OEEC becomes the Organization for Economic Cooperation and Development (OECD).
1960   The Central American Bank for Economic Integration is established.
1961   The UN General Assembly designates the 1960s as the First UN Development Decade, with two objectives: achieving an annual 5 percent growth rate in developing countries and increasing assistance to 1 percent of the combined national incomes of developed countries.
1961   France establishes a Ministry of Cooperation for independent, mainly African, developing countries.
1961   Germany begins a comprehensive development assistance program.
1961   Japan establishes the Overseas Economic Cooperation Fund.
1961   The Swiss Parliament approves a credit program for developing countries.
1961   The United States passes the Foreign Assistance Act, the basic legislation for economic assistance. The Agency for International Development and the Peace Corps are established. The Alliance for Progress, a 10-year $1 billion development program for Latin American countries, begins.
1962   The World Bank establishes a new form of donor coordination after the first consultative group for Nigeria is established.
1962   Belgium establishes an Office for Development Cooperation.
1962   The Danish Parliament establishes a secretariat for development assistance, which later becomes the Danish International Development Agency.
1962   The Norwegian Agency for International Development is established.

1963   The World Food Programme is established by the United Nations and the FAO.

1964   The first UN Conference on Trade and Development discusses trade and development problems of developing countries and recommends a target of 1 percent of national income for transfer of financial resources from each developed economy.

1964   The African Development Bank is established.

1965   The UN Development Programme (UNDP) is established.

1965   The Swedish International Development Authority is established.

1966   A legal basis for the General Agreement on Tariffs and Trade to address problems of developing countries is established.

1966   The Asian Development Bank is established.

1967   The UN Industrial Development Organization is formed.

1967   The UN Population Fund is established.

1967   The East African Development Bank is established.

1968   The Canadian International Development Agency is established.

1969   The Caribbean Development Bank is established.

1970   The UN General Assembly announces the Second Development Decade, with a target of 0.7 percent of GNP for ODA from donor countries.

1970   The Agency for Cultural and Technical Cooperation is established for French-speaking countries.

1971   The United Nations develops its first list of 25 "least developed countries."

1971   The Consultative Group on International Agricultural Research is established under the auspices of the FAO, the World Bank, and UNDP.

1971   The German government sets policy for German development assistance.

1972   The African Development Fund is established as a soft window of the African Development Bank.

1973   The Abu Dhabi Fund for Arab Economic Development, the Arab Fund for Social and Economic Development, and the Arab Bank for Economic Development in Africa are established.

1973   The Islamic Development Bank is established.

1973   The Permanent Inter-State Committee on Drought Control in the Sahel is established.

1973   The West African Development Bank is established.

1973   The UN Economic and Social Commission for Western Asia is established.

1974   The World Food Council is established by the UN General Assembly.

1974   The Asian Development Bank establishes the Asian Development Fund, a soft loan facility.

1974   Sweden becomes the first Development Assistance Committee member to achieve the 0.7 percent ODA/GNP disbursement target set by the Second UN Development Decade. The Netherlands, Norway, and Denmark follow.

1975   The World Bank opens the Third Window, which extends loans with interest rates between those of the World Bank and the International Development Association (IDA).

1975 The first Lome Convention between the EEC and African, Caribbean, and Pacific states is signed.

1975 The Central African States Development Bank is established.

1976 The OPEC Special Fund is established to channel financial assistance to developing countries on concessional terms.

1976 The Club du Sahel is created, with support from the OECD, to coordinate development aid to the Sahelian region.

1976 The Nordic Investment Bank is established.

1977 Japan launches its first doubling-of-ODA plan, which calls for disbursements to increase from $1.4 billion in 1977 to $2.8 billion in 1980.

1977 The International Fund for Agricultural Development is established.

1977 The Arab Monetary Fund is established.

1978 The World Bank publishes its first *World Development Report*, focusing on Asia and Africa.

1978 Italy establishes a Department for Development Cooperation.

1980 The UN General Assembly adopts the New International Development Strategy for the Third UN Development Decade.

1980 The World Conference of the UN Decade for Women (1976–1985) emphasizes employment, health, and education for the second half of the decade.

1980 The Food Aid Convention comes into force.

1980 The World Bank initiates structural adjustment lending designed to support changes in policies and institutions of developing countries.

1980 The Brandt Commission publishes *North-South: A Programme for Survival*.

1980 Japan launches its second doubling-of-ODA plan, increasing disbursements from $10.7 billion for the period 1976–1980 to $21.4 billion for the period 1981–1985.

1980 The World Bank and the IDA approve first operation in China for the development of higher education in science and engineering.

1983 The Brandt Commission publishes its second report, *Common Crisis: North-South Cooperation for World Recovery*.

1985 The World Bank establishes a special facility for Sub-Saharan Africa to support economic recovery and policy reforms in the region.

1985 The UN secretary-general sponsors a Conference on the Emergency Situation in Africa to mobilize $1.5 billion to help 20 drought-affected countries.

1987 At the Venice Economic Summit, seven industrial countries agree on the goal of 0.7 percent of GNP for ODA from industrialized countries.

1987 The World Commission on Environment and Development (often called the Brundtland Commission) issues *Our Common Future*.

1987 Belgium decides to increase its level of aid to meet the 0.7 percent of GNP goal by 1999.

1987 Korea establishes an Economic Development Cooperation Fund, with authorized capital of $450 million for loans to developing countries.

1988 Japan begins its fourth medium-term plan for ODA, aspiring to disburse more than $50 billion in 1988–1992 to improve its ODA-GNP ratio.

1989   The participants in the Summit of the Arch in Paris ask the commission of
        the EEC to coordinate the economic assistance of all interested countries
        to Poland and Hungary.

1989   Taiwan establishes an International Economic Cooperation Development
        Fund, with an authorized capital of $1,140 million for the provision of
        soft loans to developing countries.

1990   The UN General Assembly adopts the International Development
        Strategy for the Fourth UN Development Decade.

1990   The European Bank for Reconstruction and Development is established.

1990   A group of Soviet economic officials visits the OECD to discuss
        development aid. Hungarian economic officials visit later.

1990   The first *Human Development Report* is published by UNDP.

1991   Development assistance outlays of major donors are reoriented toward
        Central and Eastern Europe and the former Soviet Union.

1992   The UN Conference on Environment and Development is held.

□ □ □

About the Book
and Authors

Development and foreign aid are emerging as new focal points in post–Cold War international relations. Never before have economics figured so prominently in the
politics among nations; never before have individuals and nongovernmental organizations had such an opportunity to influence the success of politics in the international arena. Here, a political scientist and an economist, both with significant development experience, bring an interdisciplinary approach to the dilemmas posed
by the giving and receiving of financial and technical assistance. They answer basic
questions—What is development? Why do countries help each other develop? Who
should implement development?—while illuminating the nuances of relationships
between national and expatriate development professionals, donor and recipient
countries, and Western and alternative views of development goals. Liberally illustrated, thoroughly documented, and filled with personal anecdotes as well as cross-
national examples, the text of *Dilemmas of Development Assistance* is amplified by
suggested readings, recommended media resources, and an extensive chronology
of events marking progress in the history of development aid.

Sarah J. Tisch is the program officer at the Asian Regional Office of Winrock International Institute for Agricultural Development, Manila, Philippines, and a visiting scientist in the Social Sciences Division at the International Rice Research Institute, Los Baños, Philippines. **Michael B. Wallace,** a policy analyst at Louis Berger
International, Inc., is the chief of party for policy studies of the USAID-funded Natural Resources Management Program, Department of Environment and Natural
Resources, Quezon City, Philippines.

BOOKS IN THIS SERIES

Deborah J. Gerner
**One Land, Two Peoples:
The Conflict over Palestine**

□ □ □

Kenneth W. Grundy
**South Africa: Domestic Crisis
and Global Challenge**

□ □ □

Gareth Porter and Janet Welsh Brown
Global Environmental Politics

□ □ □

Davis S. Mason
**Revolution in East-Central Europe
and World Politics**

□ □ □

Georg Sørensen
**Democracy and Democratization:
Processes and Prospects in a Changing World**

□ □ □

Steve Chan
**East Asian Dynamism: Growth, Order, and
Security in the Pacific Region, second edition**

□ □ □

Barry B. Hughes
**International Futures: Choices in
the Creation of a New World Order**

□ □ □

Jack Donnelly
International Human Rights

□ □ □

V. Spike Peterson and Anne Sisson Runyan
Global Gender Issues

□ □ □

Index